UNCERTAIN OUTCOMES

Uncertain Outcomes

edited by

C. R. BELL, B.A., Ph.D.,
Senior Lecturer in Psychology
University of Manchester

MTP PRESS LIMITED *International Medical Publishers*

Published by

MTP Press Limited
Falcon House
Cable St
Lancaster
England

ISBN 0–85200–103–7

Photoset, printed and bound
in Great Britain by
REDWOOD BURN LIMITED
Trowbridge & Esher

Contents

List of Contributors

Leo Baric
Reader in the Department of Community Medicine, University of Manchester

C. R. Bell
Senior Lecturer in Psychology, University of Manchester

J. S. Bruner
The Watts Professor of Psychology, Department of Experimental Psychology, University of Oxford

Violet R. Cane
Director of the Manchester–Sheffield–UMIST School of Probability and Statistics and Professor of Mathematical Statistics, Statistical Laboratory, University of Manchester

Colin Cherry
Henry Mark Pease (Standard) Professor of Telecommunication, Department of Electrical Engineering Imperial College of Science and Technology, University of London

I. P. Christensen
Lecturer in Psychology, University of Manchester

Geoffrey Cohen
Lecturer in Statistics, University of Edinburgh

Sir Richard Eggleston, QC
Faculty of Law, Monash University, Australia

Johan Galtung
Project Co-ordination United Nations University, Tokyo; Professor, Institut Universitaire d'Etudes du Developpement, Geneva

Peter O. Goldblatt
Statistical Laboratory, University of Manchester

C. E. M. Hansel
Professor of Psychology, University College of Swansea, University of Wales

P. R. Meudell
Lecturer in Psychology, University of Manchester

H. T. A. Whiting
Professor and Chairman, Vakgroep Psychologie, Interfakulteit Lichamelijke Opvoeding, Vrije Universiteit, Amsterdam

As a mark of their admiration and respect,
the contributors dedicate this book to
John Cohen, Professor of Psychology
in the University of Manchester, 1952–1978,
on the occasion of his retirement.

Introduction

Except within the formal systems we invent, much of the world we inhabit and experience is characterized by some degree of uncertainty. In our past, that uncertainty may be a consequence of irretrievable loss of information. In our present, it may arise from the complexity and ambiguity of the information that bombards us. But it is in respect of our future – and its prediction – that uncertainty manifests itself most evidently.

Uncertainty is not a pleasant phenomenon to live with. Scientists may seek to attenuate their discomfort by quantifying and theorizing or model-building. Futurologists may try to reduce uncertainty through predictions based on extrapolation of 'trends' from the past. We may deal with uncertainty in our daily lives by recourse to hunches or hopes. All such activities, however, share the common feature of an involvement, in their description, of the concept of probability. The relevance of this concept to the understanding of human behaviour and thinking in the context of uncertainty is the theme of this book. The various contributors have examined the ways in which we reach decisions, respond to our environment and behave.

At the all-too-real risk of distorting the analyses which are presented by the expert contributors to this volume, an attempt may be made here to introduce a simplistic outline of the variety of probabilistic ways in which people have dealt with uncertain outcomes. Let us examine the question: 'Shall we be alive or dead tomorrow?' We could say that there is a probability of 0.5 that tomorrow we shall be alive – for the only alternative to the state of life is the state of death. This would be a mathematical probability applied to an uncertain event. It is not, strictly speaking, the mathematical probability of occurrence of an independent event – for although being alive today will not determine life or death tomorrow, if we were dead today then life tomorrow would hardly be independent of the state we are in today.

A different approach to the designation of the probability of still being alive tomorrow would be used if we regarded the outcome of tomorrow's uncertainty as being contingent upon what happens today and what has happened in the past. If we asked an insurance broker to consider our question, (s)he would attempt to calculate a statistical probability. Are we disease-free, young and living in a stable social community? Observations over many years of many disease-free, young people living in stable social communities suggest that only in exceedingly rare instances were such people dead within 24 hours. Such observations would lead the insurance broker to assign relatively low statistical probability to the prediction that we shall be dead tomorrow. Are we suicidal, smoking and drinking to excess and living in a dry timber house under a volcano on a geological fault-line? The broker's previous direct and vicarious experience of people similar to ourselves may suggest that the chances of our being alive tomorrow are somewhat low. The statistical probability of our being alive tomorrow will be estimated accordingly. But the insurance broker treats us along with other actuarial data in performing this exercise. Were we ourselves to sit down and estimate the probabilities concerned, our answers may depart quite markedly from those obtained from the broker. Both answers, however, could be expressed in similar, numerical form between a probability of 0.0 (certainty of not being alive) to 1.0 (certainty of being alive) through the region of maximum doubt, uncertainty, and unpredictability around probabilities of 0.5.

The estimate we should make of tonight's uncertain outcome would be a subjective probability. It would be 'subjective' not only because it would be about ourselves but also because we would not have access to the information available to the broker, and if we had the information it would be insufficient for us. For we *care* about the prediction we make. It is important to us in ways that are quite different from those in which it may be important to the insurance broker. Our hopes and fears may lead to over- or under-estimation of the statistical probabilities. Our belief in our own capacity to determine what happens to us may have a similar effect. Our evaluation of the ease or difficulty in arriving at the state we predict we shall be in tomorrow may affect the probability we assign to that prediction. In many ways 'oddities' may intrude into our subjective prediction of an uncertain outcome. But these 'oddities' should not be thought of as random, haphazard, inconsistent. They are 'oddities' only from the point of view of the computer-like assessors of probabilities of uncertain outcomes.

An insurance broker's *decision* to *act* in respect of the prediction of whether we shall be alive or dead tomorrow – by selling or not selling us a life insurance policy, or by fixing an appropriate insurance premium, or by inventing even more stringent limited liability clauses – will be based on as objective an assessment as possible. It would be unlikely that the decision about the action to be taken would be made without such a conscious exercise being performed first. Sometimes we, too, may postpone decisions or actions until we have performed the conscious exercise of arriving at estimates of the subjective probabilities of a variety of outcomes. But in many situations of uncertainty we do not. We decide. We act. We may be quite unaware that uncertainty exists concerning the future towards which our decisions and actions take us.

When we act or decide, cautiously or incautiously, there may be no *direct* evidence that we have estimated subjective probabilities. Yet how is an interpreter of our behaviour to achieve a model of what has happened without invoking the concept of probability assessment – unless human behaviour is to be seen as unplanned, undirected, leaping blindly into the dark? Do we not learn from our previous experience? Does not that experience in *some* way guide our decision-making, our actions? If we have expectations, they may be the result of the psychological probabilities that we carry with us.

The contents of this book reflect an interest in those personal historical, experiential, social, emotional contexts which change mathematical or statistical probabilities into subjective or psychological probabilities in models of human behaviour. Such contexts are seen to be important when people are in conditions of which the outcome is uncertain. Much of what might be identified as the 'message' of this book – although few of the contributors would welcome the ascription of a proselytizing role to them – relates to the insufficiency of current models which emphasize the rational, numerate, calculating, objective, scientific aspects of human thinking and behaviour. It is not suggested that one single model should replace another. Rather, it is suggested that a family of models may be necessary to reflect the family of aspects of human behaviour with which psychologists and others interested in human beings are concerned.

Readers may glimpse in the various chapters presented here exciting possibilities of some of the characteristics of such 'new' members of the family of models. As editor (and convert?), I have come to suspect that 'robotics' will be dead tomorrow and that 'human' psychology will be alive. I should like to express my gratitude to John Cohen for inspiring this book, and to the contributors for their most willing co-operation in its compilation. It may be seen on another page that by the unanimous wish of the contributors, this volume is dedicated to a pioneering scholar in the exploration of the concept of probability in psychology – John Cohen. Considerable editorial assistance was given by Laura Miles, Marion Elms and Jim Pavis. I should like to express my gratitude to them.

University of Manchester
April 1978 CLIFF BELL

1

Psychological Aspects of Probability and Uncertainty

C. R. BELL

In the early 1950s, when physics was king, students of experimental psychology more or less happily pursued their psychophysical investigations into shape, size and brightness constancy; into sensory thresholds – called limens if memory serves – and just noticeable differences (JNDs); and into calculations of Weber fractions or confirmations of Weber–Fechner laws.

Through such activities, the human inhabitants of psychological laboratories acquired a concept of man that reflected and emphasized his place in the physical universe. The physics of the natural world and of man, by and large, appeared to suggest that both man and his world were *log-normal*. It could be argued that, at that time, frequent recourse to logarithmic transformations of non-normally distributed human data kept Psychology firmly in the quasi-Physical, Biological Sciences rather than the Social Sciences in which the not-quite-respectable non-parametric statistical techniques flourished.

As a student of those days, Hebb had given me an exciting speculative vision of the future, Hull had provided an elegant approach to theory and Skinner had promised me a total understanding of all human behaviour – with implications about how that behaviour might be modified despite the truncation of Thorndike's Law of Effect. My view of behaviour encompassed reinforcements, generalization, fractional anticipatory goal responses. I knew that motivation concerned drive strength and goal gradients. Sensation was quite apart from perception – had I not plotted the colour zones of the human retina? And my mind was crowded with nonsense syllables (before they had aspired to a new significance as CVCs) even without my realization that I had a limited capacity channel through which they were processed.[1]

Against such a background as this, there was little chance of recognizing man as irrational, illogical, seeking, organizing, structuring, striving, self-regarding. Even Freudian concepts were being dragged out of their darkness – vainly protesting their loss of identity – into the light of the experimental psychologist's laboratory. Yet there were corners of experience that led to data which were less than easily fitted into the current physical–physiological model of man.

One such corner contained the well-tried laboratory exercise of requiring subjects to estimate their future success at a task which they subsequently performed. The subjects were then required, many times, to re-estimate their future success either for a second performance of that unchanged task or for a performance of that task made 'easier' or 'more difficult'. Changes in their *level of aspiration*[2] – as their estimate of success was called – were examined for their relation to previous performance. The experimental psychologist had no obvious explanatory problem. Verbal data (estimates of success) could be related to performance data (scores on the task) as feedback or knowledge of results – verbal behaviour being modified in accordance with the schedule of positive and negative reinforcements provided by task scores.

Hoppe (1931) had linked level of aspiration with ego-involvement. But who remembered? The shock came to the experimental psychologist when he consulted one of the 'holy' texts of the early 1950s – Hilgard (1948) – for Hilgard had written:

> Individuals tend to set momentary goals within a range of activities in which there is ego-involvement. The momentary goal is referred to as the *level of aspiration*. It is set according to the learner's interpretation of his own achievement, but there are wide individual differences in the manner of such goal-setting. . . . Those who are unrealistic may depart in either direction from their past achievements. Some are self-protective, and to avoid the possibility of failure set goals too low; others are hopeful, and set goals unrealistically too high. . . . Regardless of how one may view the conceptual system within which the level of aspiration studies are framed, it is evident that they call attention to aspects of goal-directed activities which have been neglected by those preoccupied with reward and punishment.

'Ego-involvement'? 'Interpretation of achievement'? 'Self-protective'? 'Avoid the possibility of failure'? 'Hopeful'? Such concepts as these – whatever their meaning – sounded rather too human to be psychological! Yet receptive experimental psychologists *could* be led by them not only into rich and complex seas of achievement motivation (Murray, 1938; McClelland, Atkinson, Clark and Lowell, 1953; Atkinson, 1958) *per se*, but towards the wider concept of subjective probability.

It may be that the psychophysical model of man is sufficient and appropriate for some facets of his behaviour. But for much of what he does man is not a physics-like system in an uncertain world – a point reiterated many times by the contributors to this volume. As Cohen (1972) has written:

> Man supposes, guesses and reasons; he makes estimates and inferences. He extrapolates and interpolates. He tends to generalize and make deductions. He takes risks and arrives at decisions in the light of partial information. He has dispositions and preferences. He has to deal with unique, non-repeatable as well as with repeatable situations. He has to argue from evidence to conclusion; he has to test his private hypotheses. And he has to act.

In respect of much of this, man is not the mathematician, the statistician, the scientist, nor the philosopher of logical analysis. It is perhaps within conditions of uncertainty that this is most manifest, and it is human behaviour within such conditions that is explored in this book.

SUBJECTIVE PROBABILITY IN UNCERTAINTY

In a long series of investigations, Cohen and his colleagues have sought to establish "whether judgments based on partial information follow their own psychological rules in more or less consistent fashion and how these rules compare with the rules of mathematical probability based on logical criteria" (Cohen and Hansel, 1955a). Two rather fundamental conclusions may be drawn from this body of research. The first is that in conditions of uncertainty people behave neither blindly nor randomly. The second is that in many instances human behaviour departs significantly from that which would be predicted by a model of man based on mathematical probability; for example equiprobable outcomes are not treated as such, independent events may be treated as related, preferences may be expressed where there is no mathematical justification, and concepts like hope, pessimism, or fairness may intrude.

Children's predictions of uncertain outcomes under conditions of incomplete information have been examined by Cohen and Hansel (1955a; 1955b). In one of the studies (1955a), children aged 10–14 years were required to 'guess' the colour frequency of blue or yellow beads drawn from an urn, containing unspecified proportions of beads of each colour, which were placed, without their colour being revealed to the children, into beakers. Three findings emerged from the investigation. It appeared that: (i) children assumed a roughly equal proportion of blue and yellow beads both in the urn and in the beakers; (ii) they had a marked preference for a 'balance' of outcomes in any series of beads or beakers; and (iii) there was a tendency to avoid choosing 'asymmetrical' arrangements of outcomes.

In further experiments (1955b), children aged between 6 and 14 years were tested for their ideas of independence of events. The children were asked to predict the outcome of a binary event independent of previous similar events. The preference for 'balance' was again observed in a tendency to favour the recurrence of that alternative which had been less frequently occurring in previous outcomes of these independent events. The authors suggested that there were changes in dealing with the outcome of uncertainty with increasing age such that "purely subjective preferences . . . gradually weaken and become replaced by factors inherent in the objective situation". Only in the oldest children was there an increasing number of 'either' responses to the question of which outcome was likely to happen in a series of independent binary events. Cohen and Hansel (1955a) regarded these experimental investigations as part of their study of "what we propose to call 'subjective probability'".

In the 1955 investigations, the children had no influence on the events they were concerned with. Further characteristics of subjective probability in the context of children predicting their own performance of a task were elucidated in studies reported by Cohen, Dearnaley and Hansel (1956a; 1957). In these studies, children aged 9–10 years and 13–14 years were asked to estimate how often they would succeed or fail to hit targets of various sizes in 1, 5, 10, 100, or

1000 attempts. It was found that estimates (subjective probability) of failure tended to decrease as the number of attempts to be made grew larger. Mathematically, such probabilities should have remained constant – whatever the number of attempts to be considered. Also mathematically, the sum of the children's probability of success and probability of failure should have equalled 1.0, but this was found only in respect of the subjective probabilities of success and failure involving either one attempt or five attempts. With greater numbers of attempts to be made, and especially in conditions of greatest uncertainty, the sums of subjective probability of success and subjective probability of failure were found to be less than 1.0.

The degree and influence of uncertainty with regard to the outcome of an event may depend upon two sources of uncertainty: an estimate of one's skill at the task and an estimate of chance affecting the event outcome. Cohen, Dearnaley and Hansel (1958a; 1958b) investigated the influences of these sources of uncertainty on subjective probabilities of success and failure in performance. The data obtained confirmed an earlier finding (Cohen and Hansel, 1957) that there was a reduction in the subjective probability of success when the task is perceived as easy (performers do better than they expect) and an increase in the subjective probability of success when the task is perceived as difficult (performers do less well than they expect). The studies also showed that, for adult subjects, "in a complex situation involving two sources of uncertainty, the subjective probability of success in performance is equivalent to the product of the [subjective probability of success] values relating to each separate source" (Cohen, Dearnaley and Hansel, 1958a). For children aged 12–14 years, however, "two sources of uncertainty in the same situation yield larger estimates of success than would be expected on the basis of the estimates made in two situations each with its own source of uncertainty" (Cohen, Dearnaley and Hansel, 1958b). This latter occurred whether the two sources of uncertainty were both related to estimates of skill, both related to estimates of the intrusion of chance, or a combination of skill and chance sources.

Three more findings of note emerged from these and one other related study (Cohen and Hansel, 1959). One was that combinations of two sources of uncertainty in relation to estimates of skill tend to be multiplicative in determining the combined subjective probability of success or failure, and two sources of uncertainty in relation to estimates of chance intrusions tend to be additive in determining the combined subjective probability. A second finding was that sometimes a subjective probability of success may be *greater* with two sources of uncertainty rather than one. The effect appears to be dependent upon the second, additional source of uncertainty having a larger subjective probability of success attached to it than is attached to the first source of uncertainty, and the effect is more marked as the discrepancy in the subjective probabilities of success associated with the two sources of uncertainty increases. A third major finding was that when subjects have the opportunity to choose between the sources of uncertainty, they tend to prefer to rely on the uncertainty of their skill rather than the uncertainty of chance.

Uncertainty of chance rules in lotteries. Preferences for ways of drawing a 'winning ticket' were examined by Cohen and Cooper (1961a; 1961b). In these investigations, the parameters of uncertainty in the ticket-drawing situation were systematically varied. Subjects could choose to draw from lottery ticket populations of various sizes containing the same or varying proportions of 'winning' tickets (with probabilities of between 0.01 and 0.9). They could choose to take many tickets or a single ticket from one population of lottery tickets or one or more tickets from each of several populations of lottery tickets. They could choose to try for small prizes of high probability or larger prizes of lower probability. A total of over 600 subjects was studied.

The principal conclusions that were drawn from these comprehensive investigations were: (i) a confirmation of the intransposability of choice preferences (subjective probabilities of success) across different sizes of population first reported in Cohen, Dearnaley and Hansel (1956); (ii) that when chances of drawing a winning ticket were low (0.1), subjects, in the main, tended to operate on the basis of a too-high subjective probability of success – they "concentrate on the possibilities of winning . . . look at the bright side of things, seeing it as brighter than it is"; (iii) that when the chances of drawing a winning ticket are high (0.9), the majority of subjects overestimate in their subjective probability of losing and "they concentrate on the possibility of losing . . . look on the black side of things, seeing it as blacker than it is"; and (iv) when the chances of winning and losing are equiprobable, subjective probabilities in this situation "clearly discriminate between two types of person: one with a desire to maximize the chances of success and the other with a desire to minimize the chances of failure" (*vivat* Hilgard!).

These investigations were summarized in Cohen (1964a). Other studies revealed preferences (subjective probabilities of success) for making several draws for the single winning ticket among a large population of lottery tickets than for making a single draw for the winning ticket among a small population of lottery tickets "even though the single draw was mathematically advantageous" (Cohen and Hansel, 1958). In that situation, losing tickets after being drawn had been placed back in the pool of lottery tickets. A follow-up study was later conducted in which drawn losing tickets were not put back into the population of lottery tickets from which draws were to be made (Cohen and Chesnick, 1970).

In the investigation, subjects could choose between either drawing one ticket from a small population of tickets or drawing between one and twenty tickets from a larger population of tickets. Cohen and Chesnick (1970) investigated the subjects' 'indifference point'. This was the number of multiple draws from the large population which was judged by the subjects to be a preference equal to the single draw of one ticket from the small population of lottery tickets. In only 40% of the subjects was the 'indifference point' coincident with an equivalence of the mathematical probability of success in drawing from the two populations. The remaining 60% of subjects demonstrated 'indifference points' at which either the single draw from a small population or the multiple draw from the large population was mathematically advantageous.

This did not seem to be a small 'internal standard error' of judgment phenomenon such had been discussed earlier by Cohen and Hansel (1957) and Cohen (1958a). If it had been, the indifference points of the 60% of subjects should have clustered narrowly around the point of mathematical equivalence. In fact, the indifference points occurred at almost all levels of mathematical inequivalence used in the experiments – and there was a relatively even distribution of subjects over them. As in the 1961 investigations, this 1970 study revealed that some subjects existed who tended to overvalue what were mathematically small probabilities of drawing a winning ticket. There were other subjects who tended to undervalue such probabilities. The conclusions promoted by these results – and others from a study of the effects of prior winning and losing on subsequent choices (subjective probabilities) in a roulette game (Cohen, Boyle and Shubsachs, 1969) – provided the basis for a substantial part of a review by Cohen (1970a) on the nature of gambling.

RISK AND HAZARD AS SUBJECTIVE AND OBJECTIVE PROBABILITIES

In most of the studies discussed thus far, failure following a low subjective probability of failure, or following a high subjective probability of success, could have been associated, perhaps, with a feeling of disappointment or, at most, frustration. Though participation in the investigations for some subjects on some occasions may have generated 'ego-involvement' the subjective probabilities of success or failure were attached to uncertain outcomes in relatively unemotional contexts. In a series of studies, Cohen and his co-workers have examined subjective probability as an aspect of behaviour in contexts where the participant must face hazard – "the objective probability of what will actually take place" (Cohen, 1962a) and "measured by the statistical probability of accidents" (Cohen, 1966a). In such situations, people's estimates of uncertain outcomes involve an assessment of risk – "a state of mind uncertainly contemplating what may happen" (Cohen, 1962a) arising "from subjective uncertainty of expected performance" (Cohen, 1966a).

Many aspects of subjective probability in the context of hazard and risk have been considered. Risks – and their assessment – in much of everyday life were considered by Cohen (1954) in an early paper delivered to the British Association for the Advancement of Science. Subjective probabilities of success in leaping over a beam at varying heights – when difficulty or risk was defined relatively across the individuals taking part in the experiment – were studied by Cohen and Hansel (1955c). An observational study (Cohen, Dearnaley and Hansel, 1955) of people's reaction to traffic hazards in road-crossings enabled the investigators to infer "a person's tacit beliefs about the chances of safely crossing a road, which we may regard as his subjective probability of safety (or injury)". Crossing the road at or below certain levels of subjective probability of injury – maximum risk-taking levels – varied from individual to individual but seemed to be connected with the time that would be taken by oncoming traffic to reach the crossing point. Maximum risk-taking levels – as measured in terms of times of approaching vehicles to reach the crossing point – when transformed into log seconds were found to be normally distributed for the population studied (*another* indication of our log-normal world?[3]).

In Cohen (1960), low subjective probabilities of capture, conviction by the courts, or harsh sentences were thought to be possible contributions to the unrealistically high levels of hazard accepted by criminals in pursuit of their risky activities[4]. Hazards facing motorists and their assessments of risk were examined by Cohen (1966a; 1966b). A series of reports (Cohen, Dearnaley and Hansel, 1956b; 1958; Cohen, 1958b; 1962a; 1962b) detailed investigations that had been made into subjective probability, risk and hazard in connection with the bus-driving performance of experienced and inexperienced drivers with and without the experimental variable of alcohol consumption. It was one of this series of experiments that gave rise to the now legendary account of the bus-driver who, with a blood-alcohol level of only 0.02 milligrammes of alcohol per millilitre of blood, estimated with a subjective probability of success of 0.8 that he could drive his bus through a gap which was known by him to be 14 inches (35.5 centimetres) narrower than the width of the vehicle he was prepared to drive through. He was not alone, however, for in that same study there were two other drivers who, after a modest intake of alcohol, were equally prepared to drive their 8 feet (2.44 metres) wide vehicles through gaps which they knew to be only 7 feet 5 inches (2.26 metres) wide. As Cohen (1962b) has pointed out:

> The alcohol did not disrupt their [the drivers'] performance so much as their *judgement* of their performance. We know that even under optimal conditions there is a somewhat tenuous relationship between what we *think* we can do and what we can *actually* do. After taking a little alcohol, this relationship tends to disintegrate.

Attempted and fatal suicides and suicide pacts have been examined by Cohen (1961; 1964b; 1972; 1973). The potential suicide's apparent certainty or uncertainty of outcome – his or her subjective or psychological probabilities of dying or surviving – were inferred from analyses of coroners' reports and suicide notes. In the most recent of these reports, Cohen (1973) has suggested that:

> In every case . . . there is a degree of doubt, ranging from near certainty of survival at one extreme to near certainty of death at the other. These subjective or psychological probabilities . . . may not, however, tally with the true hazards, as measured by the 'objective' probability of dying.

In the 1964 and 1973 papers, attention was drawn to the importance of psychological or subjective probabilities associated with the phenomena of 'slow-motion suicide' such as occur in patients with cirrhosis of the liver who persist in getting intoxicated, or in those who continue to be heavy smokers despite a knowledge that they risk coronary thrombosis, lung cancer or other respiratory failure. As Baric discusses later in this book, health education must be in part concerned with ways of adjusting people's psychological or subjective probabilities of potential hazards to their health in the direction of more 'objective' levels of probability; and with ways of encouraging people to set themselves thresholds of subjective or psychological probability of health hazard – maximum risk-taking levels – which will lead to health-care action on their part. Unfortunately, as health educators and Cohen (1973) are aware: "A terror which the remote future may have in store is subjectively attentuated. *When* something will happen is as decisive as *what* will happen".

UNCERTAINTY IN SEARCH

It is seldom, if ever, that human beings are not actively searching for something. They may be searching for the next correct turning in the road they travel; for a misplaced object of value; for a name to put to the familiar face that suddenly confronts them; or for a solution of tomorrow's problems. All such search is beset with uncertainties. People differ in the strategies they adopt, in the confidence they have in each step they take towards the completion of the search, in the degree of uncertainty associated with the commencement and subsequent stages of the search process, and in their estimation of the likelihood of success at the end of their search. Central to the studies of these aspects of search conducted by Cohen and his colleagues has been the question: Is human search conducted in accordance with the 'objective' or 'mathematical' probabilities that reside in the search situation?

Investigations of several different types of physical search were made by Cohen and Meudell (1968). Whilst Cohen and his colleagues have not ignored 'mental' types of search (Cohen, 1970b), the majority of their studies have been concerned with search in the world rather than with search in the mind. 'Mental' search and its theories and processes are discussed in Chapter 8 in this book, by

Meudell, but in his collaboration with Cohen, the type of search studied was that involving the location of a real or imaginary target 'out there in the world'. Data were collected on the searches conducted by children aged between 5 and 15 years. Of the major findings of these investigations, four are particularly relevant here. The authors reported that no search that they had observed had been conducted on the basis of random sampling of the search locations, even though those locations were 'objectively' equiprobable. There was a *choice* of locations for search – whatever the basis of that choice might be. Secondly, it might be expected that the subject's confidence in the correctness of his next guess as to the correct location of the target might increase as incorrect locations were eliminated from the total population of locations. As this did not appear to happen, the authors concluded that psychological probability – "the confidence of a subject in the accuracy of his guess" – seemed to have little basis in the 'objective' probability characteristics of the search situation. A third outcome of the investigations was that no children below the age of 7 years – and few at that age – adopted a search strategy involving a classification, grouping or set of potential locations of the target. However, as their fourth major finding indicated, "even a young child will not make an exhaustive exploration of every place in which an object may be hidden. He will somehow limit himself to those few places which seem to him subjectively promising". The search strategies adopted by the subjects appeared to be influenced by psychological rather than 'objective' probabilities, both at the beginning of the search as well as throughout its course; and "these two kinds of probability are not isomorphic".

Confirmation of the tendency of subjects to impose a pattern of unequal probabilities onto a population of mathematically equiprobable locations was clearly shown in three experiments conducted by Cohen, Boyle and Chesnick (1969). The importance of the concept of 'subjective information' in search discussed by Cohen and Meudell was amplified in a study of visual search in which subjects aged between 7 and 10 years showed a progressive improvement in their 'mental efficiency' in the performance of search task – defined as fewer search steps becoming associated with more 'bits' of information – with increasing age (Cohen, Boyle and Chesnick, 1971).

Examination of the strategies adopted by 14- and 15-year-olds in a multi-stage search task led to a discovery invested with considerable importance by the investigators Cohen, Chesnick and Haran (1971;

1972). It was found that in multi-stage search tasks, the compound mathematical probabilities (products of the mathematical probability of correct guessing or sub-goal attainment at each individual stage) of location of the target of the search were almost invariably less than the overall subjective or psychological probabilities of success at the task used by the subjects. People expected to perform better than was mathematically probable, as they had done in the single estimations of their performance in earlier studies (Cohen and Hansel, 1957; Cohen, Dearnaley and Hansel, 1958a; 1958b).

The significance of this finding and its relevance to the search for solutions in protracted multi-stage negotiations, for decisions in complex, multi-facet situations, or for the overcoming of a succession of obstacles, led Cohen, Chesnick and Haran (1971) to give it the "special designation" of the 'inertial psychological probability effect'. Later, these authors (1972) described the 'inertial psychological probability effect' as possibly a "characteristic feature of human judgement" and suggested that if we

> assume that our experiment simulates a variety of situations in daily life, as in administrative, medical, industrial, military and other professional contexts, where an individual has to make a number of consecutive choices or decisions, with an element of chance entering at each stage . . . we may expect the decision-maker to err in his strategy or judgement by the overvaluation of his chance of making a correct choice at every stage. In general, the more stages, the greater the error of judgement.

CONCLUDING REMARKS

If there is one important conclusion to be drawn from the body of research reviewed here – and it is confirmed in many of the other chapters in this book – it is that behaviour in uncertainty, which may include the vast majority of human behaviour, disputes the appropriateness of a model of man which emphasizes a rational, physics-like system. Human beings, in their preferences, judgements, decisions and actions, appear to be rather more psychological than mathematical; rather more 'subjective' than 'objective'; and rather more of the world inside their head than in the 'real' world outside.

Cohen (1965) has expressed something of this view – which is echoed later in this book by Cherry (Chapter 6) – in a reference to:

> the different types of theoretical models of choice which have been proposed. Those that come from mathematical statisticians tend to be based on the assumption that the decision-maker is a rational man, or at least a very reasonable one, and indicate the strategies which should be followed for the best pay-off. . . . Models preferred by psychologists relate to *actual* choice behaviour, and it can be shown that such behaviour is not readily intelligible on the assumption that the chooser is a sophisticated robot.

If, however, there is one important element missing from the body of research reviewed here – and to some extent its absence is remedied in some of the later chapters in this book – it is the recognition that much of human behaviour is social behaviour. In Chapter 7, for example, Bruner calls attention to the limits of "decision theories that concentrate upon the lonely, endopsychic mental life of the individual".

It appears, from a review of the literature, that neither Cohen and his colleagues, on the one side, nor the majority of social psychologists, on the other, were aware of how an exchange of ideas may have brought benefit to both. With some temerity, this particular product of the psychology of the early 1950s would suggest that Cohen's views on subjective and psychological probability might be read with interest by psychologists concerned with social comparison theory. He would further suggest that Festinger's (1954) seminal paper on social comparisons – and all the research that grew from it into predictions of performance, levels of confidence, the need to evaluate one's own abilities, etc., etc. (Harvey and Smith, 1977) – could be read with interest by those probability theorists who, like Cohen, have seen non-robotic man living in an uncertain world, and coping with it.

NOTES

1. The presentation of this view has had to be a simplification amounting to an exaggeration. Lest those responsible for my psychological education be hurt, let me admit receiving a fuller education than is implied here. Any psychology laboratory which had lead-shot pellets cheek by jowl with Thematic Apperception Tests or galvanic skin response apparatus could not be too bad! But my memory of the significant part of the 1950s is still Hebb (1949), Hull (1943) and Skinner (1938; 1953).

2. The concept of level of aspiration did not die. It may have flourished in the 1940s but it is still alive in the 1970s (see: Lewin, 1935; Sears, 1940; 1941; Frank, 1941; Lewin, Dembo, Festinger and Sears, 1944; and Fontaine, 1974).

3. Although the idea of a log-normal world is expressed here only semi-seriously, it ought not to be forgotten that such an idea may have been a stimulus to the development of 'natural' logarithms – if a footnote in Fisher and Yates (1948) is to be regarded as significant.

4. I discussed this aspect of Cohen's work with a friend, Evelyn Ruse, who had just returned from a 1968 Summer Workshop on 'Mass communication and motivation: Family planning' at the University of Chicago. In the context of her association with both the Family Planning Association and the International Planned Parenthood Federation, we debated whether a reluctance on the part of prisoners and their spouses, or among disturbed adolescents, to make use of family planning aids could derive, in part, from a similar misperception of risk and hazard.

BIBLIOGRAPHY

Atkinson, J. W. (ed) (1958). *Motives in Fantasy, Action, and Society: A Method of Assessment and Study.* (New Jersey: Van Nostrand)

Cohen, J. (1954). Conjecture and risk. *The Advancement of Science Reports of the British Association*, **11**, 333–339

Cohen, J. (1958a). The measurement of uncertainty. *Discovery*, **19**, 286–290

Cohen, J. (1958b). The effect of alcohol on risk-taking. *Proceedings of the XIII Congress of the International Association of Applied Psychology* (Rome)

Cohen, J. (1960). *Chance, Skill and Luck.* (Harmondsworth: Penguin)

Cohen, J. (1961). A study of suicide pacts. *The Medico-Legal Journal*, **29**, 144–151

Cohen, J. (1962a). Strategic considerations in the study of road traffic and alcohol. *Proceedings of the Third International Conference on Alcohol and Road Traffic.* (London)

Cohen, J. (1962b). Alcohol and road accidents. *Triangle: Sandoz Journal de Sciences Medicales*, **5**, 214–220

Cohen, J. (1964a). *Behaviour in Uncertainty.* (London: Allen & Unwin)

Cohen, J. (1964b). Forms of suicide and their significance. *Triangle: The Sandoz Journal of Medical Science*, **6**, 280–286

Cohen, J. (1965). Preference, choice and money values. *Discovery*, July, 19–23

Cohen, J. (1966a). The motorist's ordeal. *New Scientist*, 17 February, 402–403

Cohen, J. (1966b). Patterns of accidents and possibilities of prevention. *Proceedings of the Second Congress of the International Association for Accident and Traffic Medicine*, pp. 81–94 (Stockholm)

Cohen, J. (1970a). Idea of search. *Schweizerische Zeitschrift für Psychologie und Ihre Anwendungen (Revue Suisse de Psychologie Pure et Appliquée)*, 66–75 (Festschrift für Richard Meili)

Cohen, J. (1970b). The nature of gambling. *Scientia: Revue Internationale de Synthèse Scientifique*, **105,** Juillet/Août, 1–25

Cohen, J. (1972). *Psychological Probability or the Art of Doubt.* (London: Allen & Unwin)

Cohen, J. (1973). Death pacts. *Medikon International*, No. 9, 17–23

Cohen, J., Boyle, L. E. and Chesnick, E. I. (1969). Patterns of preference in locating targets. *Occupational Psychology*, **43,** 129–144

Cohen, J., Boyle, L. E. and Chesnick, E. I. (1971). An experimental study of visual search. *Ikon*, **76,** 1–15

Cohen, J., Boyle, L. E. and Shubsachs, A. P. W. (1969). Rouge et Noir: influence of previous play on choice of binary event outcome and size of stake in a gambling situation. *Acta Psychologica*, **31,** 340–352

Cohen, J. and Chesnick, E. I. (1970). The doctrine of psychological chances. *British Journal of Psychology*, **61,** 323–334

Cohen, J., Chesnick, E. I. and Haran, D. (1971). Evaluation of compound probabilities in sequential choice. *Nature (London)*, **232,** 414–416

Cohen, J. Chesnick, E. I. and Haran, D. (1972). A confirmation of the inertial- effect in sequential choice and decision. *British Journal of Psychology*, **63,** 41–46

Cohen, J. and Cooper, P. (1961a). Patterns of preference in equiprobable situations. *Nature (London)*, **190,** 231–232

Cohen, J. and Cooper, P. (1961b). A model for choice in equiprobable situations. *Acta Psychologica*, **18,** 181–200

Cohen, J., Dearnaley, E. J. and Hansel, C. E. M. (1955). The risk taken in crossing a road. *Operational Research Quarterly*, **6,** 120–128

Cohen, J., Dearnaley, E. J. and Hansel, C. E. M. (1956a). The addition of subjective probabilities: The summation of estimates of success and failure. *Acta Psychologica*, **12,** 371–380

Cohen, J., Dearnaley, E. J. and Hansel, C. E. M. (1956b). Risk and hazard: Influence of training on the performance of bus drivers. *Operational Research Quarterly*, **7,** 67–82

Cohen, J., Dearnaley, E. J. and Hansel, C. E. M. (1957). Measures of subjective probability: Estimates of success in performance in relation to size of task. *British Journal of Psychology*, **48,** 271–275

Cohen, J., Dearnaley, E. J. and Hansel, C. E. M. (1958a). Skill and chance: variations in estimates of skill with an increasing element of chance. *British Journal of Psychology*, **49,** 319–323

Cohen, J., Dearnaley, E. J. and Hansel, C. E. M. (1958b). The mutual effect of two uncertainties. *Durham Research Review*, **2,** 215–222

Cohen, J., Dearnaley, E. J. and Hansel, C. E. M. (1958c). The risk taken in driving under the influence of alcohol. *British Medical Journal,* **1,** 1438–1442

Cohen, J. and Hansel, C. E. M. (1955a). The idea of a distribution. *British Journal of Psychology,* **46,** 111–121

Cohen, J. and Hansel, C. E. M. (1955b). The idea of independence. *British Journal of Psychology,* **46,** 178–190

Cohen, J. and Hansel, C. E. M. (1955c). Experimental risk-taking. *Jahrbuch für die Psychologie und die Psychotherapie,* Winter

Cohen, J. and Hansel, C. E. M. (1957). La répartition des probabilités subjectives. *Journal de Psychologie Normale et Pathologique,* Janvier–Mars, 10–21

Cohen, J. and Hansel, C. E. M. (1958). The nature of decisions in gambling: equivalence of single and compound subjective probabilities. *Acta Psychologica,* **13,** 357–370

Cohen, J. and Hansel, C. E. M. (1959). Preferences for different combinations of chance and skill in gambling. *Nature (London),* **183,** 841–842

Cohen, J. and Meudell, P. (1968). Strategies of search. *Acta Psychologica,* **28,** 322–343

Festinger, L. (1954). A theory of social comparison processes. *Human Relations,* **7,** 117–140

Fisher, R. A. and Yates, F. (1948). *Statistical Tables for Biological, Agricultural, and Medical Research,* 3rd edn. (Edinburgh: Oliver & Boyd)

Fontaine, G. (1974). Social comparison and some determinants of expected personal control and expected performance in a novel task situation. *Journal of Personality and Social Psychology,* **29,** 487–496

Frank, J. D. (1941). Recent studies of the level of aspiration. *Psychological Bulletin,* **38,** 218–226

Harvey, J. H. and Smith, W. P. (1977). *Social Psychology: An Attributional Approach.* (St. Louis: C. V. Mosby)

Hebb, D. O. (1949). *The Organisation of Behaviour: A Neuropsychological Theory.* (New York: Wiley)

Hilgard, E. R. (1948). *Theories of Learning.* (New York: Appleton-Century-Crofts)

Hoppe, F. (1931). Erfolg und Misserfolg. *Psychologische Forschung,* **14,** 1–62

Hull, C. L. (1943). *Principles of Behaviour.* (New York: Appleton-Century-Crofts)

Lewin, K. (1935). *A Dynamic Theory of Personality* (translated by D. K. Adams and K. E. Zener). (New York: McGraw-Hill)

Lewin, K., Dembo, T., Festinger, L. and Sears, P. S. (1944). Level of aspiration. In J. McV. Hunt (ed): *Personality and the Behaviour Disorders.* (New York: Ronald Press)

McClelland, D. C., Atkinson, J. W., Clark, R. A. and Lowell, E. L. (1953). *The Achievement Motive.* (New York: Appleton-Century-Crofts)

Murray, H. A. (1938). *Explorations in Personality.* (Oxford University Press)

Sears, P. S. (1940). Levels of aspiration in academically successful and unsuccessful children. *Journal of Abnormal and Social Psychology*, **35,** 498–536

Sears, P. S. (1941). Level of aspiration in relation to some variables of personality: clinical studies. *Journal of Social Psychology*, **14,** 311–336

Skinner, B. F. (1938). *The Behaviour of Organisms: An Experimental Analysis.* (New York: Appleton-Century-Crofts)

Skinner, B. F. (1953). *Science and Human Behaviour.* (New York and London: Macmillan)

2

Subjective Probabilities and Statistical Parameters

GEOFFREY COHEN

This paper is addressed to psychologists whose interest in subjective probability centres primarily on data of a statistical nature and not on probability assessments of a unique kind, such as betting on an election result. The first three sections are non-technical although some familiarity with probability and statistics is assumed. After a very brief sketch of subjective and non-subjective views of probability, some psychological aspects and difficulties are illustrated by means of an example. The following section mentions some empirical psychological work and tentatively suggests some directions for future studies. The last two sections assume a rather fuller acquaintance with statistics. The place of the subjective (or Bayesian) approach in statistics is briefly surveyed in the fourth section. The final section sets out some objections to the most complete statement of the subjective view as given by de Finetti.

NOTIONS OF PROBABILITY

The intriguing nature of probability is a subject in which philosophy, natural science, mathematics, statistics and psychology all have a part to play. Some people contend that several distinct notions must be distinguished; others that there is a single unifying notion, or that only one of the notions proposed has any real meaning. Hacking (1975), in an outstanding monograph, has clarified the origins of the essential duality in the concept of probability – on the one hand *epistemic*, relating to our knowledge and beliefs, and on the other hand *aleatory*, relating to the physical characteristics of 'chance set-ups' which exhibit stable long-run frequencies. To the psychologist the study of probability as conceived by human minds merges with the study of vaguer notions conveyed by such words as 'doubt' and 'possibility'. John Cohen (1972) gives a fascinating survey of these less precise areas which are nevertheless crucial to a fuller understanding of the subject.

The epistemic side of probability takes its foremost modern guise in the theory of 'subjective' or 'personal' probability. An individual is assumed to be willing to bet on the truth of a verifiable proposition. His behaviour when presented with various hypothetical gambles can be used to define his degree of belief in the proposition. The mathematical theory shows that if certain axioms of rational behaviour are accepted then the subjective probabilities so defined must obey the usual rules of mathematical probability. From a purely inferential viewpoint the theory purports to show exactly how a person's beliefs should be modified in the light of experimental data: by means of Bayes' theorem (Bayes, 1763). The theory is of course a normative one, telling us how the idealized 'rational man' should behave, and a variety of different axiomatizations have been proposed which attempt to embody the concept of rational behaviour. In some weaker versions subjective probabilities may be only partially ordered, or it may only be possible to show that 'upper' and 'lower' probabilities exist (Smith, 1961; Suppes, 1974). In other words these versions formalize the idea that not all degrees of belief may be comparable, or that a person may only be able to place bounds on his degree of belief rather than state an exact value. But in practice a version of the axioms strong enough to ensure completely ordered exact probabilities is generally preferred.

A rather different but nevertheless epistemic interpretation of probability has been advanced by Keynes (1921) and Jeffreys (1939). This is the 'necessary' or 'logical' view which sees probability as the unique degree of belief which any rational man with a given body of knowledge would hold in the truth of a proposition. Although the works of these two writers, particularly those of Jeffreys, have had a profound influence on philosophers and statisticians, they are perhaps of less concern to psychologists. This is partly because, in the most interesting cases, people's bodies of relevant knowledge do differ, though to an extent which is impossible to delineate precisely, and hence their subjective probabilities may not agree.

The aleatory aspect of probability is formalized through the concept of long-run relative frequency. The first modern attempts at a satisfactory definition are usually attributed to Venn, and can be traced through von Mises to more recent statisticians and philosophers. While the philosophers have struggled mightily to wrest a satisfactory formalization from this difficult concept, statisticians and other scientific users of probability have for the most part been satisfied to ignore the serious foundational problems while maintaining that some kind of frequency interpretation of probability is the only approach both practicable and meaningful for their work. The philosophers attempt to circumvent the difficulties of long-run relative frequency by explaining aleatory probability as a *propensity*, or *dispositional property*, of a 'chance set-up'. Such a set-up may be thought of as something akin to an urn full of balls together with a defined sampling procedure which will yield unpredictable results on repeated draws but will exhibit some kind of long-run stability for the relative frequencies of different results. This approach can be traced back to the classical definition of probability in terms of the number of 'favourable cases' out of a set of 'equally possible' or 'equally likely' cases. Here 'possibility' may be thought of as an early version of the notion of 'propensity'.

Amongst the adherents to a subjective view of probability there are those, such as de Finetti (1973), who regard all philosophical attempts to explicate the aleatory side as unsuccessful, and others, probably the majority, who simply see the scope provided by the aleatory view as too limited. The latter, then, are prepared to admit two different kinds of probability into their scheme of things: one an objective physical property of certain 'set-ups' to be measured, in some sense, by relative frequency; and the other a subjective degree of belief, either about different possible 'set-ups' (only one of which in fact exists) or about some unique 'trial' (such as an election); the degree of belief being measured either directly by questioning, or, more usually, indirectly by the implications of a person's betting preferences.

Some form of this dual view is also held by many practising statisticians and scientists who would probably never regard themselves as subjectivists. An interesting case is that of Fisher (1956), who introduced the apparently epistemic notion of *fiducial probability* for dealing with hypotheses, while vigorously maintaining the existence of objective physical probabilities for the processes under observation. The meaning of fiducial probability, *qua* probability, has never been very satisfactorily explained, but as a mode of inference the fiducial argument has continued to hold a fascination for many statisticians, and has even made something of a comeback of late.

AN EXAMPLE

There are circumstances in which most people would agree on the most appropriate interpretation of probability. For instance in radioactive emission it is natural to conceive of the long-run rate of decay as a physical constant quite independent of any subjective assessments of probability, and of the probability of an emission in a given time-interval as related in some sense to this long-run physical property. For phenomena of this kind few people would concur with de Finetti's view, that all reference to the 'purely metaphysical' objective probability is unnecessary if only we analyse the situation through the concept of exchangeability. An interesting critique of this view is offered by Hacking (1965, p. 213). In contrast we have applications of probability in business decisions, such as the marketing of a completely new product. It is only natural here to take a subjective view, since no long-run interpretation of the uncertainties involved can carry much conviction. Whether one chooses to use the term 'probability' for the quantifications of belief that are commonly used in such situations is largely a matter of taste. In order to clarify some of the issues I wish to raise I will consider an example intermediate between the two extremes outlined, and yet typical of many problems, particularly in the social sciences.

When insuring a house against fire an insurance company needs to assess the probability of fire within the space of, say, a year. Of course, different kinds of fire with more or less serious consequences need to be considered, but for simplicity let us assume that fire is an all-or-nothing event. Some kind of long-run frequency is clearly relevant, but it is by no means clear whether it is the frequency of fires in all houses, the frequency of fires in houses of a particular age and type, the frequency of fires in houses occupied by persons of a particular age and socioeconomic group or some other frequency. If we classify the house and occupier according to every possible particular we come down to the unique individual case and are left with no frequency at all, but the considerable problem of assigning a subjective probability to the event of fire in this unique case. The problem is a fundamental one: what other cases should be regarded as statistically compatible with the one to hand, or, in different terminology, what is the fundamental reference set?

The practical reply will be that this depends on what data are available or feasible to collect: we will classify by as many as possible of the relevant explanatory variables and then use the appropriate relative frequency as our estimate of probability for the house in question. But several objections may be raised. First there will doubtless be some knowledge pertaining to the unique case that we consider relevant to the chance of fire but for which no frequency data are available. Should not this knowledge be utilized somehow to 'improve' the probability assessment? Secondly, even if no such knowledge exists, it is clear that the house in question has not been selected from any group by a physical procedure akin to a chance set-up. On what grounds therefore may we identify the probability for the unique case with the relative frequency in a group of 'similar' cases? Some kind of subjective assessment, not only of what constitutes 'similarity' but of symmetry between similar cases, is clearly at work and should perhaps be brought into the open. Thirdly the more finely we characterize the house (i.e. the more explanatory variables we allow), the smaller will be the group of 'similar' cases, and hence the less reliable will be any estimate of statistical frequency that we adopt. Fourthly, it is not entirely clear how we should decide whether an explanatory variable is relevant, and the answer to this question may perhaps depend on our conception of probability.

The absence of an obvious fundamental reference set is regarded by subjectivists as a good example of how meaningless it is to speak of an objective probability of fire with a frequency interpretation. According to them any individual insurer must weigh up for himself the probability of fire for the particular house in question, taking into account all factors he considers relevant, including any available statistical data on frequency of fires. Moreover in this view the relation of the subjectively assigned probability to any known statistical frequency is sufficiently explicated by the theory of exchangeable events.

But the psychological question of how the assessment is made is left open. The normative mathematical theory gives no clue as to how to choose an appropriate group of 'similar' cases or how to use any special information about the unique case in a quantitative way to 'adjust' an observed frequency. What some proponents of the theory recommend is that the insurer himself consider how he would react if certain kinds of further information were available. To borrow Lindley's words (1971) he should "extend the conversation". A careful probability assessment for the particular house should be consistent not only with the weight he attaches to all the relevant information to hand, but also with the weight he thinks he would attach to any kind of relevant future information that he can conceive. Equally he should reflect on the probability assessments he would give for other particular houses and ensure that they too are consistent with his present assessment. In short, it is vital to assess subjective *conditional* probabilities, conditional not only in the obvious sense on the information to hand, but also on hypothetical other information that might modify one's assessment.

To illustrate these ideas let us suppose that the company has data from a reasonably long series on the relative frequency of fires in houses of different ages and on the relative frequency of fires according to the socioeconomic group of the head of household ('the occupier') but that the relative frequency in houses classified according to both variables simultaneously is not known. If house age and occupier's socioeconomic group were considered to be the only relevant variables which affect the chance of fire then the assessed probability for the particular house would be equal to the unknown relative frequency of fires in the group of houses similar to the given house on *both* variables. Commonly however there will be further relevant information for the particular house for which corresponding statistical data are lacking. For example the fabric and structure of the house may be thought by the insurer to be a better than average risk even though the company has no adequate historical records to support such a belief. Formally the problem may be set out as follows:

Let

- E be the proposition that a house will have a fire within the next year;
- X be the proposition that a house is of age x, the age of the given house;
- Y be the proposition that a house is occupied by persons of socioeconomic group (SEG) y, the SEG of the occupier of the given house;
- Z be the proposition that a house is of structure and fabric similar to that of the given house.

Let XY denote the conjunction of propositions X and Y and let $P(X|Y)$ be the conditional probability of X given Y. Then we require an assessment of $P(E|XYZ)$ where we have some statistical data relevant to $P(E|X)$ and $P(E|Y)$, and also a non-statistical belief that $P(E|Z) < P(E|\bar{Z})$ where $\bar{Z}$ is the complement of Z. The incomplete character of this problem, with certain vital information lacking, reflects a difficulty commonly encountered in practice.

An important psychological point to note in passing is the ease with which different conditional probabilities may be confused. If, for example, there is an association between X and Z, so that it is difficult to think of a house of age x which does not have a fabric like the given house, then $P(E|X)$ may be easily mistaken for $P(E|XZ)$. It is also very easy to confuse the conditioning and conditioned events, e.g. to mistake $P(X|Z)$ for $P(Z|X)$. We shall return to this theme in the next section.

The best way to ensure an assessment that really reflects our beliefs is not only to try and iron out confusions directly but also to 'extend the conversation' to many other probabilities with which we are not directly concerned. This is because the numerical values we assign to the probabilities required will inevitably imply relations between the probabilities of other propositions in the algebra generated by E, X, Y and Z. Having assessed the required probabilities we may find that we have, by implication, assigned a value to some other probability that does not really accord with our beliefs. We will then have to rethink our original assessments so as to remove this inconsistency. For example the following relation must hold between our assessed probabilities of fire for houses of type XYZ and $XY\bar{Z}$:

$$\frac{P(E|XYZ)}{P(E|XY\bar{Z})} < \frac{P(XY|\bar{Z})}{P(XY|Z)}$$

The probabilities on the right-hand side could perhaps be assessed from a knowledge of the housing situation quite independently of any consideration of fires. We could then check whether our assessed fire probabilities on the left-hand side satisfied the relation.

To be genuinely realistic we should have to insist on consideration of probabilities for houses of all different ages, structures and occupiers, comparing them with our probability for the house in question and revising where necessary until we were satisfied that our beliefs were truly reflected in the numbers given. Although the whole example is rather artificial it will perhaps convey the essence of the message. A wider discussion of many of the points is given by de Finetti (1974).

Before leaving the example we will consider it briefly from a non-subjective point of view, partly in order to highlight certain differences and partly to bring out some points that have so far remained in the background. For instance, precisely how should the observed past frequency of fires in houses of age x be related to $P(E|X)$? It may be noted that the definitions of E, X, Y and Z refer somewhat loosely to 'a house' and not to the particular house in question. Equating the probability of fire for a given house aged x with the corresponding past frequency is equivalent to saying: if we know nothing about a particular house other than that its age is x, and if we know that the frequency of fires in houses of age x is f, then a reasonable degree of belief in E for this particular house is just f. This form of expression is much closer to the logical view of probability than it is to the subjectivist. For a subjectivist any degree of belief is reasonable provided it is consistent with other beliefs held. The fact that a degree of belief may conform to some known frequency is, in a sense, secondary and is held to be explicable by the theory of exchangeability.

To attempt a frequentist account of the problem we restrict ourselves, to start with, to the single explanatory variable, age. We must argue that the chance of fire in houses of age x is in some sense a physical property determined by the average condition of such houses and the multifarious fire hazards they contain. Each fire in such a house is then viewed as the outcome of a random process analogous to those in more familiar chance set-ups such as coin-tossing. The varied nature of real houses makes this interpretation seem very stretched, for why should one house of age x be similar to another in the way that one toss of a coin is similar to another? The answer must either rest upon the unconvincing supposition that no other explanatory variables exist, or upon a belief that whatever other variables are involved are in some sense 'distributed at random' among houses of age x.

A slightly more sophisticated account would be as follows. We may suppose that if all the major explanatory variables (or 'causes') that affect the chance of fire were known, then in the class of houses within which all these variables were constant the outcome of fire for any one house would be strictly akin to an outcome in a chance set-up. (This argument still views the remaining 'minor' explanatory variables as 'distributed at random' so that nothing is really clarified; but the alternative, in an objective view, would be complete determinism.) In so far as no explanatory variables other than age are known or controlled we may regard the event of fire as the outcome of a two-tiered set-up. The first tier would be the 'drawing' of a genuine chance set-up out of all those with value x for the explanatory variable age, while the second tier would be the 'drawing' of the outcome fire from the genuine chance set-up selected. The first tier cannot however be regarded as a genuine chance set-up, since the uncertainties involved in it arise solely from our lack of knowledge of the other explanatory variables.

Under an interpretation of this kind there is a 'true' value for $P(E|X)$ given by an expression of the form:

$$P(E|X) = \int p(x,y,z)f(x,y,z) \quad \mathrm{d}y\,\mathrm{d}z,$$

where we assume that:

(i) there are just two other explanatory variables, y and z;
(ii) there is a genuine objective probability $p(x,y,z)$ for houses with values x, y and z on the three explanatory variables; and
(iii) the frequency function $f(x,y,z)$ represents the distribution of the three explanatory variables in the population of all houses.

In order to relate $P(E|X)$ to the observed past frequency we also need to assume that:

(iv) the sample of houses on which the observed frequency is based is in some sense a 'random sample' from the population of houses with frequency function $f(x,y,z)$.

The above is by no means a full account, and may not even be a fair account, of a frequentist interpretation for our example. But whatever precise form this interpretation may take, one practical way in which it will differ from a subjective interpretation is that the observed past frequencies of fires in houses of age x will be recognized as an estimate of some unknown parameter, and a measure of the error in the estimate may well be calculated. This contrasts strongly with the subjective view, for although it may make some intuitive sense to speak of having greater or lesser confidence in our subjective probability assessments, it is difficult to attach a meaning to the notion that they are in error – except in so far as they may be inconsistent with one another in the manner described earlier.

PSYCHOLOGICAL ASPECTS OF THE SUBJECTIVE APPROACH

We have mentioned in the previous section some of the confusions that are likely to arise when assessing subjective probabilities. An elegant series of experiments by Tversky provides many further examples of mistakes of different kinds, and illustrates some of the mental heuristics used by people to assess probabilities.

In one experiment, "subjects were shown brief personality descriptions of several individuals, allegedly sampled at random from a group of 100 professionals" (70 engineers and 30 lawyers). "The subjects were asked to assess, for each description, the probability that it belonged to an engineer rather than a lawyer" (Tversky, 1974). The relative odds that an individual is an engineer (E) rather than a lawyer (L), given his description (D), may be expressed as the ratio

$$\frac{P(E|D)}{P(L|D)}$$

which is mathematically equal to the product

$$\frac{P(D|E)}{P(D|L)} \left| \frac{P(E)}{P(L)} \right.$$

But when given a description that was apparently completely uninformative $(P(D|E) = P(D|L))$, subjects reported even odds rather than the odds of 7 : 3 which would result if the information contained in the 'prior probabilities' or 'base rate frequencies' were taken into account. On the other hand when no descriptions at all were available subjects reported the 'correct' odds. It would appear that when confronted with the descriptions, albeit uninformative, subjects were unable to distinguish $P(E|D)$ from $P(D|E)$. No-one who has attempted to teach elementary statistics will be unfamiliar with this kind of mistake.

Tversky characterizes results such as these as judgment by 'representativeness' or 'similarity'. In his view when asked for the probability that an object *A* belongs to a class *B* or that an event *A* originates from a process *B*, "people typically compare the essential features of *A* and of *B* and assess the degree of similarity between them, or the degree to which one of them is representative of the other" (Tversky, 1974; p. 149). The probability that a personality description originates from an engineer is assessed by evaluating the similarity between the description and the stereotype of 'an engineer', while prior probabilities play no role. A further feature of this heuristic is that, in evaluating the similarity between a sample statistic and a population value, the role of sample size is obscured. The probability of obtaining a deviation of given magnitude from the population value is assessed by subjects independently of sample size. Thus the expectation that a small sample will be highly representative of its parent population is apparently common, even among experienced users of statistics.

A related way of looking at this phenomenon is in terms of a tendency to assume a 'random distribution' for an explanatory variable, or, more accurately, to assume that the particular values taken by such a variable for the units under study are somehow equivalent to ('exchangeable with', 'sampled at random from') the other values that might obtain. This attitude may be illustrated among psychologists themselves by their neglect of random sampling in their researches. While many psychologists may simply regret the unfortunate fact that the majority of psychological experiments are carried out on a very restricted class of subjects, usually students (Cochrane and Duffy, 1974), there are some, such as Eysenck (1975), who repudiate the desirability of testing hypotheses on a sample of subjects selected at random from some population. Underlying such an attitude seems to be the belief (or faith?) that the important explanatory variables are 'randomly distributed' in some population, or at any rate that they are not correlated with observable variables which could be used to define a population and take a random sample from it. Just as Tversky's subjects, when distracted by the 'information' in a description, seem to ignore or forget about the patently relevant prior probabilities $P(E)$ and $P(L)$, and implicitly to assume they are equal, so may a psychological investigator, engaged by the phenomenon under study, forget about some special characteristics peculiar to his subjects, which make his findings difficult to generalize, without some assumptions about the distribution of these characteristics in a larger population.

This tendency to assume an underlying 'random distribution' for explanatory variables, whenever it is convenient for drawing inferences, is so widespread and deep-rooted that it seems a worthy subject for psychological exploration. It plainly manifests itself in a variety of ways – we saw in the previous section how it would figure in an objective account of the insurance example. Sometimes the assumption is of a uniform distribution, that is all possible values of the explanatory variable are assumed equally probable, but more often it is simply assumed that the values obtained can be treated as though they were a random sample drawn from the set of all possible values. Yet there are also situations where the opposite phenomenon is displayed – a tendency to believe in the existence of some deliberate pattern where no evidence for such a pattern exists. As an example we may cite one of John Cohen's experiments where subjects were asked to guess the location in an array of circles of the 'magic circle' that the experimenter was thinking about. There was a marked preference for certain areas of the array which seems to indicate a non-uniform distribution of belief over the array (Cohen and Christensen, 1970).

Before passing on to suggest some other directions of enquiry for research into probability assessments, it may be useful to consider the difference in approach between mathematical statisticians on the one hand and psychologists on the other. The statisticians have principally been interested in developing pay-off schemes which encourage people to report their beliefs honestly, and in training people to avoid mistakes in their assessments (i.e., to avoid assessments which lead to an improper probability distribution). By contrast psychologists have been concerned not only with getting honest and proper assessments, but also with the mistakes themselves and the psychological reasons for them. Psychologists have also devoted effort to comparing subjective assessments with the 'correct' objective probabilities for standard chance set-ups such as coin tossing, dice throwing and the like. To the statisticians these enquiries are of little interest, partly because, as far as the normative theory is concerned, any assessment is 'correct' so long as it is consistent with other assessments, but mainly because they believe it most important to elicit probabilities in realistic situations. The standard chance set-ups are rather artificial, and the subjects in such psychological experiments have little prior information to draw on and little motivation to reflect hard about their assessments. But in the sort of enquiries recommended by the statisticians, business managers are confronted with relatively realistic uncertainties about which they should have considerable background information, however intangible. It is felt that such situations encourage a more thoughtful attitude on the part of the subjects since they are expected to be more genuinely interested in the accuracy of their assessments.

One particular line of psychological research has emphasized the inadequacy of human beings as information processors. The idea has been to compare a person's successive probability assessments, as data are accumulated, with those provided by an application of Bayes' theorem. This is an example of comparing responses with normative as opposed to an objective standard. It has been amply demonstrated that, in general, people are 'conservative' in their revision of subjective probabilities – they do not adjust them in the light of the data as much as they should according to Bayes' theorem. A reaction to this finding from some mathematical statisticians has been to call for better training, so that people will conform more closely to the normative standard; yet it may be questioned whether this Bayesian standard does indeed encompass fairly the idea of rationality. Suppes (1966; 1974) has argued that it does not, as has Hacking (1965; 1967). One major objection is to the way in which the subjective theory derives Bayes' theorem for application to 'revision' of probabilities. If a person is considering a series of trials, say coin tosses, then a full Bayesian analysis requires that he assign a subjective probability to all possible sequences of future outcomes; and hence, implicitly at least, he must assign probabilities to future outcomes conditional on other future outcomes, e.g. a probability that the $(n+1)$th toss will be a head if the first n tosses turn out to be heads. But this does not imply that once n tosses have been carried out he must stick to his former opinion. To be self-consistent he should, but he may, in the meantime, have had further opportunity for reflection, or have been apprised of some new relevant information, or conceived an entirely new theory to account for the results of coin tosses. To change his mind for any of these reasons would not, on the face of it, appear irrational, although it does imply a lack of consistency between opinions held at different times. The 'rationality' of the subjective theory, which is restricted to self-consistency among probability assessments, applies, strictly speaking, only to assessments made at a given point in time, including any *contemplated* future conditional probabilities.

The root of the objection is to any stipulation that a person stick rigidly to the assessments made at one time about future events. The presumption in the theory, as applied to statistical situations, is that the person reflects very carefully to start with, bearing in mind all factors he considers relevant, before coming to a probability assessment. Induction in the light of accumulated data then proceeds quite mechanically by means of Bayes' theorem. But such a prescription seems rather far removed from our real mental processes, save perhaps for such well-understood set-ups as coin tossing. We very often think as we go along, and knit together initial beliefs and observational data in a highly unstructured, 'back-and-forth' kind of way. We must conclude that the normative Bayesian standard is far too rigid to serve as a psychological model for probabilistic learning. Findings such as 'conservatism' are primarily of interest for those who believe in the existence of objective chance set-ups, and want to train people to learn about them more effectively.

A more psychologically constructive response by statisticians to the research on 'conservatism' would be to look for non-Bayesian models of human probabilistic processing. A start has been made (Goldblatt and Cane, 1976) but much further work remains. On the psychological side I would like to suggest that attention be directed towards assessment of conditional probabilities and away from the traditional sequences of independent (or exchangeable) events. In the decisions of everyday life, where application of subjective probability ideas is most fruitful, statistical dependence is the norm rather than the exception.

Turning briefly then to decision theory, the rigidity of the normative Bayesian approach can again be criticized. An optimum decision, in terms of maximum expected utility, is of course optimum only if the decision structure chosen is appropriate. What seems characteristic of real decision problems is the great variety of ways in which they can be formalized. Sometimes the way in which the terminal decisions themselves should be characterized is open to doubt. More commonly there is considerable choice in the structure of the decision tree, in deciding whether some branches should be split up into smaller branches, others collapsed together into a single 'large' branch. If, for example, I wish to sell my car, I may, to begin with, consider a few prices offered by recognized dealers. Going one step further I may consider an expected price if I hawked it round a larger set of dealers. Similarly I may think of selling it privately, and after obtaining some information from newspaper advertisements, I may consider an expected price from a private deal. Then again I may think of 'doing the car up' before selling it. Various levels of expenditure (or expected expenditure) in this direction could be combined with a new assessment of expected gain from either or both of the above types of sale. And so on – the problem may be extended indefinitely. The question is really one of choice of model, and as such the criticism of 'rigidity' applies to model-building of any kind and not just to the Bayesian approach. But because the Bayesian approach apparently embraces so many elements: possible decisions, possible states of nature, probabilities of different outcomes, utilities of different consequences, we are perhaps more easily lulled into thinking we have the 'right' answer when using it rather than some less ambitious approach. By attempting to take everything into account it tends to make us forget those things which have not been included in the model. Certainly criticisms of this nature have been made in statistics, and in economics similar comments have been made about cost–benefit analysis. What we ultimately have to face is that however much model-building clarifies our thinking, no formal process can match the flexibility of the mind in selecting the elements of a problem and arranging and rearranging them.

As far as probability assessments in decision problems are concerned, the psychology of such assessments is vastly more complicated than some theorists would have us believe. Attitude to risk has been acknowledged as a problem since the time of Bernoulli, but beliefs in the effect of luck (the ability of some outside agency to affect outcomes), and the effect of skill (the ability of the individual to affect outcomes) are also of great interest. The explorations of John Cohen (1960; 1964; 1972) are, I believe, of pioneering importance in this field. While statisticians, logicians and economists evolve a normative standard of rational thought and behaviour, it is, in his view, the psychologists' task to describe the real man, whose probability assessments are characterized by such irrational beliefs as luck.

I would like to conclude this section by suggesting that some psychological attention be given to comparing probability assessments, obtained by careful questioning about all branches of a compound decision tree, with the 'unitary' assessments obtained when the decision tree is collapsed down into a very simple structure. It is my view that when evaluating uncertainties for decision-making we may often be relatively accurate without knowing 'how we got there'.

We do not go in for much mental model-building and when asked to evaluate a conditional probability from somewhere along the tree we may find difficulty in replying accurately. In addition, as hinted earlier, our response may be rather different from that we would give if we had actually reached that point in the tree. To give a crude example, I may be able to give a relatively accurate expected price for my car, and possibly some probabilities for different prices, without deciding who I am going to sell it to or whether I am going to do it up first. If I break the problem down into these components one would expect my final assessments to be more accurate; but will they be? The difficulty of assessing the increase in selling price to be derived from an investment of £100 in doing it up may introduce 'errors', or greater uncertainties, into the final result. It is surely a matter of empirical psychology to investigate whether improving the detailed formulation of a model results in any greater accuracy in the overall conclusion.

In making these comments I am clearly thinking of an objective frequency standard for evaluating the 'accuracy' of probability assessments. Such evaluations have been employed by subjectivist statisticians, particularly in relation to weather forecasting, and could in principle be adapted for the kind of investigation I have in mind. If indeed these conjectures have any worth there would be important repercussions for model-building. I do not wish to denigrate model-building, only to suggest that the psychology of such processes is an interesting study in itself.

THE BAYESIAN APPROACH IN STATISTICS

De Finetti (1973) has quite rightly drawn attention to the distinction between statisticians who merely employ Bayesian techniques and those who adopt a wholeheartedly subjective viewpoint. While no hard and fast line can be drawn I shall consider first the viewpoint of those Bayesians (the majority) who appear to believe in the objective validity of the statistical models that they study, but regard the Bayesian approach as the most appropriate for drawing inferences about their models. Later I shall mention the more extreme subjectivism of de Finetti, who comes to grips with the many philosophical problems swept under the carpet by the former approach but, in my opinion, fails to solve them satisfactorily.

The typical setting for much of statistical inference is as follows. Observational data are taken to be generated by some 'random', or 'stochastic', process whose mathematical description involves certain unknown parameters. It is desired to draw inferences about the values of the parameters or to take decisions whose consequences depend on these values. The inferences are typically in the form of a test of hypothesis or a point or interval estimate. Orthodox frequentist statistics prescribes various procedures for making estimates or performing tests which have desirable long-run properties. For example in the standard linear model least-squares estimators may be shown to have minimum variance among all linear unbiased estimators. Bayesian techniques on the other hand start with a prior probability distribution for the unknown parameters. This distribution is taken to incorporate the (possibly unformalized) knowledge and opinions of the person doing the study about the process under observation. The observational data enter into the calculations via the likelihood function, which simply expresses as a function of the unknown parameters the probability of obtaining those observations that were actually made. The prior and likelihood are combined, by means of Bayes' theorem, to produce a posterior distribution for the unknown parameters. All Bayesian inferences are based on this distribution which is taken to combine, in an appropriate way, prior and extraneous information with that contained in the observational data, and to provide subjective probabilities that should be attached, in the light of the data, to any possible parameter value or set of values. Although, as described here, Bayesian methods appear appropriate only to parametric statistical inference, we may note in passing that the Bayesian net has, in fact, been cast much wider; even covering such apparently unpromising areas of statistics as non-parametrics and sampling theory.

Among the reasons advanced by Bayesians for dissatisfaction with the orthodox approach we may note the following. First and foremost is the feeling that what is wanted, at the end of the day, is a statement of epistemic probability about the unknown parameters. The frequentist approach, by definition, is unable to deliver the goods. For example, Neyman's careful frequency definition of confidence intervals is regarded by many Bayesians as a piece of tortuous semantics which, in practice, goes by the board: the confidence level being almost universally treated as an epistemic probability to be conferred on the particular interval obtained.

Secondly the criteria by which frequentist procedures are chosen are, to a large extent, *ad hoc*. One procedure will usually fail to satisfy all the desirable criteria. For example a maximum likelihood estimator may not be unbiased, or a likelihood ratio test may not be uniformly most powerful. In general many frequentist procedures violate the likelihood principle. This entails that conclusions should depend only on the probability of obtaining those observations that were actually made, the probability of obtaining any other observations being considered irrelevant. By contrast the conclusions derived from frequentist procedures usually depend on the manner in which the data were collected, and hence take into account the probabilities of all possible observations. From a decision-theoretic point of view a recommended frequentist procedure may often be inadmissible, in the sense that some other procedure will be superior whatever the values of the unknown parameters. Bayesian procedures are, however, always admissible, given a proper prior distribution, and in fact it can be shown that all admissible procedures are Bayesian with respect to some prior distribution.

Thirdly we may mention as a source of dissatisfaction the philosophical problems associated with the concepts of aleatory probability and independence, although this is more properly considered as a motivation of the 'extreme' subjectivists than of the typical Bayesian statistician.

In contrast to the above, the positive advantages of the Bayesian approach are felt to be:

(i) a conclusion in the form of a clear and concise statement of epistemic probability – the posterior distribution;
(ii) an explicit way of incorporating useful prior information into a statistical procedure, which also clearly exposes the influence of personal beliefs;
(iii) a general framework for all statistical problems, both purely inferential ones and decision problems.

In connection with (iii) we should note that many problems traditionally treated by orthodox statistical methods, such as hypothesis testing, are felt by Bayesians to be more properly formulated as decision problems.

We must now consider some of the difficulties associated with the Bayesian approach. Foremost amongst these is the problem of specifying a prior distribution. The problem is particularly acute when a person has little or no prior information. The original Bayesian approach, the so-called 'method of inverse probability', which held sway from the time of Laplace until well into this century, fell into disrepute precisely because of its uncritical use of uniform prior distributions to represent ignorance. The underlying 'Principle of Insufficient Reason' was questioned by philosophers, while Fisher based his attack on the grounds that uniform priors are not invariant under transformations of the parameters. For example, complete ignorance of the value of θ might be thought equivalent to complete ignorance of the value of θ^2; but a uniform probability distribution for θ, over a finite range, implies a non-uniform distribution for θ^2. The modern Bayesian defence to this is that there is really no such thing as complete ignorance – there is always some prior information, however vague. In so far as extremely vague priors are required, structural arguments can be put forward for choosing the particular function of the parameter that is to be given a uniform distribution. But, in general, a uniform prior should be defended as a positive statement of equal prior belief in all parameter values, rather than being defended by the Principle of Insufficient Reason. In any case the influence of a vague or diffuse prior is easily swamped by an informative likelihood, so that with any reasonable number of observations the posterior distribution is little affected by the precise form of the prior. Nevertheless the use of improper priors (e.g. a uniform distribution over an infinite range) has recently been found to lead to paradoxes in multi-parameter problems (Dawid, Stone and Zidek, 1973).

Whatever the extent of prior information, the pragmatic Bayesian practice of choosing the form of prior distribution on the basis of mathematical convenience is clearly open to criticism. Even more questionable is the not entirely uncommon practice of choosing the form of the prior in the light of the data.

We have no more than sketched a few of the pros and cons of the Bayesian approach. There are plenty of good arguments in favour of more orthodox approaches which probably account for their continued overwhelming popularity. For a fuller discussion of the statistical issues see Cox and Hinkley (1974) and Barnett (1973). We can, however, consider the more general objection to combining subjective prior beliefs with the objective information supplied by the data. For those who hold an overtly dual view of probability there is little justification in combining the two kinds or probability into a composite posterior distribution. While few statisticians would deny the importance of considering all relevant prior information, many would question the propriety of formally combining, on an equal footing, as it were, the subjective uncertainties with which an investigator starts and the objective measure of uncertainty yielded by the observations. Combining two different kinds of probability also lacks a firm logico-philosophical basis. While the frequentist and subjective approaches are both buttressed by a large body of philosophical writing and axiomatic development, there are few philosophers who have attempted a complete account of how the two approaches could be combined.

Thus, to the extent that the typical Bayesian statistician accepts his parametric models as objective he is a dualist and lacks a philosophical foundation on which to rest his combination of subjective and objective probabilities; but to the extent that he regards the probabilities in his models as subjective – and hence directly comparable with his subjective prior beliefs – he becomes what I would term an 'extreme' subjectivist, and this leads, I believe, to further difficulties.

SOME OBJECTIONS TO 'EXTREME' SUBJECTIVISM

One of the foremost proponents of a consistently 'extreme' subjectivism has been de Finetti. He denies the existence of any objective, physical probabilities and regards the language of frequentist theory as couched in 'metaphysical obscurity'. The fundamental frequentist notion of a series of independent, identical trials (Bernoulli trials) with a constant probability of 'success' is rejected – or, rather, it is re-analysed through the notion of exchangeability.

A person is said to regard a series of trials as exchangeable if he assigns probabilities to the series of outcomes in such a way that the order of outcomes is unimportant to him. (Technically, the joint distribution of the outcomes of a set of k trials depends only on k and not on the positions of the k trials in the series.) Given such an assignment de Finetti's famous representation theorem shows that the probability, $p(m,n)$, assigned by the person to any series of $m + n$ trials comprising m successes and n failures, can be expressed in the form:

$$p(m,n) = \int_0^1 \theta^m(1-\theta)^n \, p(\theta) \, d\theta \quad \text{where} \quad p(\theta) > 0 \quad \text{and} \quad \int_0^1 p(\theta) \, d\theta = 1. \qquad (1)$$

Here $p(\theta)$ has the properties of a probability density and is, in fact, the density implicitly ascribed, prospectively, to the limiting frequency in an indefinitely long series of trials.

It is important to remember that de Finetti regards it as meaningless to speak of this limiting frequency as a fixed but unknown physical parameter of the process generating the trials. Because the person does not know in advance what the relative frequency of success will be in, say, n future trials, it is for him a 'random quantity' and he can assign a probability distribution to the possible values it may take. The fact that, given exchangeability, this distribution tends, in the limit for large n, to a (continuous) probability distribution with density $p(\theta)$, means that he is effectively assigning a probability distribution to the limiting frequency that will be realized, although, strictly speaking, limiting frequencies do not exist. The status of θ in equation (1) is thus somewhat paradoxical. On the one hand the person may regard it as a random variable whose probability distribution is approximately that he would assign to the relative frequency of success in a large number of trials. But on the other hand he should not regard it as being a parameter, or probability, characteristic of the whole process and 'applying', in some sense, to every trial of the series. The probability assigned to success on any given trial of the series is the mean of the distribution characterised by $p(\theta)$ (as can be seen by putting $m = 1, n = 0$ in (1)). Alternatively we may say that the person's expectation of the long-run frequency ('prevision' in de Finetti's terminology) must equal the probability he assigns to success on any given trial.

The import of equation (1) may be described in the following way. If a person views a series of trials as exchangeable, then the probability he assigns to any event in the sample space of all possible sequences is the same as that he would assign if he regarded the series as generated by a two-stage procedure: first a selection of a 'physical' probability θ according to the distribution $p(\theta)$, and then a series of independent trials with constant probability θ. Hence, it is argued by Bayesians, the probability the person would wish to assign to a success at the $(m + n + 1)$th trial after observing the $m + n$ trials comprising m successes and n failures may be worked out by the person in an analogous way: first by thinking of a density function $p(\theta)$ which reflects his initial opinions about the long-run frequency of success, and then by calculating,

$$Pr \text{ success at } (m+n+1)\text{th trial} \mid m,n) = \frac{p(m+1,n)}{p(m,n)}$$

$$= \frac{\int_0^1 \theta^{m+1}(1-\theta)^n\, p(\theta)\, \mathrm{d}\theta}{\int_0^1 \theta^m (1-\theta)^n\, p(\theta)\, \mathrm{d}\theta}$$

$$= \int_0^1 \theta\, p(\theta \mid m,n)\, \mathrm{d}\theta \qquad (2)$$

where $p(\theta \mid m,n)$ is the 'posterior density' for θ after observing m successes and n failures.

Equation (2) is the fairly standard form in which Bayesian inference for the 'parameter' of a Bernoulli process would be presented in textbooks. With some sleight of hand the function $p(\theta)$ becomes a prior density for a 'parameter' θ, although the starting point of the argument was to deny the existence of any real quantity corresponding to θ. The sleight of hand lies first in saying that Pr (success at $(m + n + 1)$th trial $\mid m,n$) is worked out from $p(\theta)$ and second in pretending that the parameter θ has some fixed objective value. The argument given above, although innocuous at first sight, is suspect because it loses one of the most appealing aspects of the subjective theory – the strictly behavioural definition of probability. So long as we stick to probabilities like $p(m,n)$ (that is to probabilities of events in the sample space) we are essentially asking the person to consider bets about a finite sequence of trials. Such bets can easily be imagined and there is, at least, no conceptual difficulty in defining $p(m,n)$. But as soon as we talk of probabilities like $p(\theta)$ we are asking the person to consider bets about a very long, essentially infinite, sequence of trials. Since such bets can never be realized in a finite time the whole exercise begins to lose touch with reality. For this reason it seems to me far more satisfactory to say that a person is asked for his probabilities $p(m,n)$, for various m and n (and from these, if desired, an approximate $p(\theta)$ may be deduced), than to say that a person is asked for his probability density $p(\theta)$ and that from this may be deduced future conditional probabilities like Pr (success at $(m + n + 1)$th trial $\mid m,n$).

As we have already hinted, the distinction is further clouded in practice since Bayesians usually try to assess a prior distribution for a 'parameter', representing the 'probability of success'. If taken literally such a demand seems either to entail accepting what was denied from the start – the existence of a real, constant, unknown probability which applies at every trial – or to be asking for a distribution of prior belief about a subjective probability, that is for a distribution of 'second-order' probabilities. If not entirely meaningless, 'second-order' probabilities are at the very least hard to define behaviourally, for it is difficult to conceive of betting about one's own betting preferences. Our conclusion, then, should be that to remain true to the subjectivist spirit prior distributions should be recognized as having for their arguments not 'parameters' but unknown (and in that sense random) long-run frequencies.

Unfortunately it is extremely difficult for a statistician to adhere to such a stipulation. We are mentally conditioned to thinking in terms of parametric models, and however much we would like to concentrate on prediction about future events, rather than inference about unknown parameters, it is difficult to conceive of ever doing away with parameters. Indeed it is hard to see how understanding, as opposed to prediction, could advance except through such models. The natural way for a Bayesian to tackle a statistical problem is to set up a prior distribution for the parameters. But in so far as the values of the parameters, whether thought of as fixed unknown quantities or simply as long-run averages of future observations, can never be known with certainty this means that the hypothetical bets on which the prior distribution is based are unrealistic.

The above account is not entirely fair in that there are some situations where even an extreme subjectivist can legitimately give a physical interpretation for a parameter. Consider, for example, random sampling without replacement from an urn with K balls, of which M are red and the rest black. Let the outcome of the ith draw from the urn be denoted by the random variable Y_i, taking the value 1 if the draw results in a red ball and 0 otherwise. A subjectivist translation of the phrase 'random sampling' would be that the Y_i are considered exchangeable by the person doing the sampling. If this person is prepared to consider K draws, all exchangeable, then for him,

$$Pr\,(Y_1 = 1) = E(Y_1) = E(Y_2) = \ldots = E(Y_K) = \theta, \text{ say},$$

where $E(Y_i)$ denotes expectation (or 'prevision'). It follows, since coherence implies that his expectations obey the usual mathematical rules, that

$$K\theta = E(Y_1) + E(Y_2) + \ldots + E(Y_K) = E\left(\sum_{i=1}^{K} Y_i\right)$$

But it is certain that

$$\sum_{1}^{K} Y_i = M,$$

the total number of red balls in the urn, and hence

$$E\left(\sum_{1}^{K} Y_i\right) = M \text{ and so } \theta = M/K.$$

Thus the probability assigned to obtaining a red ball on any one draw must equal the proportion of red balls in the urn, a perfectly plain physical parameter. Now, by analogy with equation (1), the probability $p(m,n)$ assigned to getting a sequence of m red balls and n black ones in some order, can be represented as:

$$p(m,n) = \sum_{\theta} H_{m,n}(\theta)\, p(\theta) \tag{3}$$

where $H_{m,n}(\theta) = \binom{K\theta}{m}\binom{K-K\theta}{n} \Big/ \binom{K}{m+n}\binom{m+n}{n}.$

$H_{m,n}(\theta)$ is the ordinary probability that would be derived according to classical probability arguments.

Our objection above to arguing from $p(\theta)$ to $p(m,n)$ now loses its force. We can perfectly well define $p(\theta)$ in terms of conceptual bets about the unknown proportion of red balls in the urn, and there is nothing inherently unrealistic about such bets, since they no longer require an infinite time to be realized. For expository purposes de Finetti (1975; p. 218) obtains equation (1) as the limit of equation (3) as $K \to \infty$. Although the mathematics is quite acceptable it conceals, in my view, a disturbing change, as one passes to the limit, in the psychological realism of the desired interpretation of the theorem.

Whatever may be thought of this plea for a degree of realism in the bets which underlie subjective probabilities, there is a growing tendency among Bayesians to move in the opposite direction. This is shown in the practice of introducing 'hyper-parameters' and 'hyper-hyper-parameters', which can best be illustrated by an example. Suppose that a person is interested in making an inference about the mean θ of some normally distributed observations. If he finds it difficult to specify precisely his prior distribution for θ then it is suggested (Lindley and Smith, 1972) that he should express it in terms of a further unknown 'hyper-parameter', e.g. $p(\theta)$ might be normal with mean ξ. Then, ξ being unknown, he will be obliged to specify a prior distribution for it – possibly involving further unknown 'hyper-hyper-parameters' – and so on. Notwithstanding the mathematical convenience of this device it seems clear that the psychological assessments required to implement it are far removed from the simple bets which serve for the usual definitions of subjective probability.

Comments on de Finetti's views on different lines have been made by many writers. Hacking (1965) gives a philosophical rejoinder to the claim that objective probabilities are unknowable and therefore purely illusory. Good (1965) argues that the notions of independence and constant physical probability are psychologically prior to exchangeability, in that one would not accept the latter unless the former were already at the back of one's mind. This seems to me a valid point although it is hard to see how it could be tested. Hamaker (1977) claims that an exchangeable series of trials is indistinguishable from an independent series with constant probability. He also believes that, however exchangeability may account for the stability of long-run frequencies within a single series of trials, it cannot account for the reproducibility of results in different series, which is the essence of scientific work. To sum up, few people appear to espouse wholeheartedly the extreme subjectivist viewpoint of de Finetti. Nevertheless his highly original mathematics, and stimulating philosophy, have made an outstanding contribution to thinking in this field.

BIBLIOGRAPHY

Barnett, V. D. (1973). *Comparative Statistical Inference.* (London: Wiley)

Bayes, T. An essay towards solving a problem in the doctrine of chances. *Philosophical Transactions of the Royal Society,* 1763, **53,** 370–418

Cochrane, R. and Duffy, J. C. (1974). Psychology and scientific method. *Bulletin of the British Psychological Society,* **27,** 117–121

Cohen, J. (1960). *Chance, Skill and Luck.* (Harmondsworth: Penguin)

Cohen, J. (1964). *Behaviour in Uncertainty.* (London: Allen and Unwin)

Cohen, J. and Christensen, I. P. (1970). *Information and Choice.* (Edinburgh: Oliver and Boyd)

Cohen, J. (1972). *Psychological Probability or The Art of Doubt.* (London: Allen and Unwin)

Cox, D. R. and Hinkley, D. V. (1974). *Theoretical Statistics.* (London: Chapman and Hall)

Dawid, A. P., Stone, M. and Zidek, J. V. (1973). Marginalization paradoxes in Bayesian and structural inference. *Journal of the Royal Statistical Society, Series B,* **35,** 189–233 de Finetti, B. (1973). Bayesianism: its unifying role for both the foundations and the applications of statistics. *Bulletin of the International Statistical Institute*, **45(4)**, 349–367

de Finetti, B. (1974). *Theory of Probability*, Volume 1. (London: Wiley)

de Finetti, B. (1975). *Theory of Probability*, Volume 2. (London: Wiley)

Eysenck, H. J. (1975). Who needs a random sample? *Bulletin of the British Psychological Society*, **28**, 195–198

Fisher, R. A. (1956). *Statistical Methods and Scientific Inferences*, (3rd edn 1973). (Edinburgh: Oliver and Boyd)

Goldblatt, P. O. and Cane, V. R. (1976). Experiments on choice under uncertainty and their analysis. Manchester–Sheffield School of Probability and Statistics, Research Report

Good, I. J. (1965). *The Estimation of Probabilities*. (Cambridge, Massachusetts: MIT Press)

Hacking, I. (1965). *The Logic of Statistical Inference*. (Cambridge University Press)

Hacking, I. (1967). Slightly more realistic personal probability. *Philosophy of Science*, **34**, 311–325

Hacking, I. (1975). *The Emergence of Probability*. (Cambridge University Press)

Hamaker, H. C. (1977). Subjective probabilities and exchangeability from an objective point of view. *International Statistical Review*, **45**, 223–231

Jeffreys, H. (1939). *Theory of Probability*. (2nd edn 1948). (Oxford: Clarendon Press)

Keynes, J. M. (1921). *A Treatise on Probability*. (London: Macmillan, 1921; reprinted New York: Harper, 1962; London: Macmillan, 1973)

Lindley, D. V. (1971). *Making Decisions*. (London: Wiley)

Lindley, D. V. and Smith, A. F. M. (1972). Bayes estimates for the linear model. *Journal of the Royal Statistical Society, Series B*, **34**, 1–41

Smith, C. A. B. (1961). Consistency in statistical inference and decision. *Journal of the Royal Statistical Society, Series B*, **23**, 1–37

Suppes, P. (1966). Probabilistic inference and the concept of total evidence. In J. Hintikka and P. Suppes (eds) *Aspects of Inductive Logic*. (Amsterdam: North-Holland)

Suppes, P. (1974). The measurement of belief. *Journal of the Royal Statistical Society, Series B*, **36**, 160–175

Tversky, A. (1974). Assessing uncertainty. *Journal of the Royal Statistical Society, Series B*, **36**, 148–159

3

Distributional and Non-distributional Uncertainty

I. P. CHRISTENSEN

The pursuit of 'objectivity' (*via* the Scientific Method) in the study of human behaviour during the post-war era had amongst other things the effect of shifting the emphasis of research towards those aspects of human behaviour which were readily observed and quantified. There appeared to be some feeling that perhaps the emulation of the methods by which the inanimate world had been so successfully studied might lead to discoveries of regularities in human behaviour which could in turn lead to accurate predictions of future behaviour being made. Psychologists were looking for 'Laws'.

In some notable cases this approach proved to be extremely profitable. To be sure some of the Laws turned out to be a little less than immutable, but in the repealing of them more knowledge was gained and more stable theoretical edifices were erected. There were, however, costs to be borne. Firstly many facets of human behaviour were, and are, intrinsically unsuited to experimental study. Simulations of 'real life' situations in a laboratory may not be so convincing that the participants behave as they would in normal circumstances. Subjects may not be able to emit the required behaviour at will. The presence of an investigator may irretrievably alter the situation, or the experiments which seem to promise the most informative results may be out of the question because of ethical considerations; and so on. Thus many areas of human behaviour were ignored by researchers although the pioneer psychologists allowing their imagination freer reign (and some, incidentally, displaying considerable wisdom) had thought them proper subjects of study.

Secondly the search for explanations brought with it another kind of problem. The nature of explanations in psychology has been thoroughly discussed elsewhere (e.g. Meredith, 1964) and it is evident that explanations for behaviour can be proffered on several levels. The simplest of these is merely a restatement of data in new terms, for example words or other symbols. If this is cunningly done it may be possible to infer the nature of further behaviour which would be evoked by different experimental conditions, but any such predictive power derives from the rules which govern the manipulation of the chosen symbols rather than from any deeper understanding of psychological processes which their use has afforded. Examples of such 'explanations' would be theories of intelligence or personality based on factor analytic techniques (Spearman, 1927; Cattell, 1957).

A different and more complex kind of explanation comes from the invention of a hypothetical mechanism which would produce the observed behaviour. These mechanisms are usually simple diagrams drawn on paper, and they are intended to be *functionally equivalent* to psychological mechanisms, but not necessarily *structurally equivalent*. Perhaps one of the most famous of these models is Broadbent's early (1958) description of the mechanism of attention. One of the strengths of this approach is that the elements of the model (for such it is) often have properties other than those strictly necessary for the explanation, and by using these properties predictions may again be made about the behaviour of people in specified circumstances. These predictions, viewed as hypotheses, are then subjected to experimental test. If they turn out to be true then the model is retained for further examination, otherwise modification, or even rejection, of the model is called for.

The importance of these models in shaping the way in which researchers think about a problem cannot be overestimated, and nowhere is this more evident than when the model is not a novel construction, tailored to the behaviour in question, but an *analogy* drawn between that behaviour and the behaviour of some other functionally similar system which is better understood. In such a case the prime system (which provides the model) may become a normative standard against which the performance of the secondary system (in this case human psychological mechanisms) is judged. Taken to the limit there will be a temptation to conclude that human beings are inferior kinds of mechanisms rather than to admit that the prime system is a poor model.

The mathematical theory of probability is a case in point. Many authors have for a long time regarded probability theory as providing a normative model describing the way in which people *should* behave in uncertain situations, and there is no denying the force of this assertion in some circumstances. A prudent man will not ignore probability theory when seated at a roulette table (but then again would a prudent man be in a casino anyway?); a sober economist can make accurate forecasts of investment income, and he can also perpetrate immense blunders. We shall argue that, rather than judging human behaviour to be faulty with regard to the theory, we should judge the theory to be an inadequate explanation of behaviour.

SHORTCOMINGS OF THE MODEL

In general one may distinguish at least four distinct interpretations of the term probability. These are usually referred to as the classical, frequency, logical and subjective definitions (Cohen and Christensen, 1970) but only the first two, the *classical* and the *frequency* interpretations have a place in the mathematical theory.

The *classical* interpretation is primarily attributed to Bernoulli (1713). He defined probability as the proportion of favourable outcomes in the set of all possible and equally probable outcomes. If there are n equally probable outcomes the probability, p, of each of them is $1/n$. If m of them are favourable then the probability of a favourable outcome is m/n. This definition is manifestly circular, as has often been observed, for the idea of probability is already assumed in the undefined expression 'equally probable outcomes'.

The *frequency* interpretation avoids this circularity, omitting any reference to equiprobability. Probability is simply defined as the limit of the relative frequency of the outcomes of an event within a set of outcomes. For instance the statement 'the probability that a person can drive a car is 0.4' means simply that if we were to take increasingly large samples of people we would find the proportion of car drivers coming closer and closer to four in ten.

Probability (defined in either of these ways) can be regarded as a variable expressing uncertainty as to the truth of an hypothesis. It seems clear, however, that people do not often behave in the manner suggested by these definitions; the data of human experience do not, on the whole, comprise the right kind of stuff. If someone decides to apply for a new job thinking that they 'will probably get it', this judgement does not imply either the classical or the frequency definition. Yet much of human activity involves choices, and perhaps the sharpest contrast between the idea of probability as a relative frequency and the reality of human uncertainty is to be found in the kind of choices which Shackle (1961) has called *self-destructive experiments*. These are cases in which someone is faced with several courses of action in a situation unique to his experience. The outcome of each alternative is uncertain but he must choose one, and any choice is irrevocable in the sense that, once made, the situation (and/or the individual) is so changed that repeat 'experiments' to determine the frequency with which each alternative has the desired outcome are not possible. One cannot un-declare a war, un-read a book or be un-rude to one's superior at work. If you crash your car swerving to avoid something in your path, you cannot go back and see if applying the brakes might not have been a better idea! We are not, of course, denying that people learn from experience, but simply saying that bringing experience to bear at the moment of choice is a long way from the kind of situation in which a frequency probability may be calculated; yet it is a common enough type of situation.

Although this shortcoming alone rules out the productive use of probability as an uncertainty variable in many situations there is another point to be made, for in rejecting models it is useful to know all of their failings so that new ideas may avoid old pitfalls.

It is implicit in either of the definitions of probability set out above that the numerical values of the probabilities assigned to each member of a set of mutually exclusive and exhaustive outcomes of an event must sum to unity. The probability that one of the outcomes will occur is 1.0, and this probability is said to be *distributed* over the alternatives. In many choice situations, however, a person may not be sure that he is aware of the complete set of outcomes. It would not then be feasible to assign a set of numbers reflecting that person's relative uncertainty about the alternatives such that those numbers sum to unity. There may be another outcome which properly deserves a share, and ignorance does not (on the formal definitions) excuse us from ignoring it, although in practical terms it may be difficult to see how we could do otherwise. An obvious solution to this problem might seem to be to lump together all the unknown potential outcomes and assign a probability to that subset without further differentiation, but really this would be of little help. If we do not recognize these alternatives as belonging to the set of outcomes, presumably we have never observed them before as an outcome of the event in question. That being so we have no data upon which even to guess at what fraction of unity would be appropriate to express our uncertainty.

A further problem emerges if we consider in what sense a probability-value can be regarded as 'knowledge'. Let us not forget that in no sense is a probability-value a property of the outside world[1]. It is not so much the world that is uncertain as our ability to predict it. In this sense all probabilities are psychological in that they refer to states of people's minds. Now as Shackle (1961) has remarked, knowledge and uncertainty are mutually exclusive. If someone entertains more than one hypothesis about the future state of the world then it is implicit that one of them may be wrong. A probability value used to denote this uncertainty only constitutes knowledge about the past, because it expresses the relative frequencies with which things have been observed to occur. In looking to the future we must assume that the conditions under which these observations were made will persist and that things will continue as they have done.

If this is true, one may object, how is it that the insurance business (to pick one of many enterprises) flourishes as it does? The answer to such a question lies at the heart of the contention that probability is an unsatisfactory uncertainty-variable for much of human behaviour. Consider the two hypotheses 'I will live through tomorrow' and 'I will not live through tomorrow'. They are mutually exclusive, and may be thought of as *rivals*. Which of them is true is of crucial importance to me, but irrelevant to an insurance company which is not concerned with predictions about particular individuals. Their actuarial data are not applicable to my hypotheses at all; their hypotheses concern only the proportions of their clients who will die, and *both* of my hypotheses will be compatible with theirs.

Probability, as defined for the purpose of mathematics has, then, inherently strong limitations for the description of individual uncertainty. If we wish to understand human behaviour in such circumstances we must seek fresh ideas.

NON-DISTRIBUTIONAL UNCERTAINTY

The biggest problem to be overcome in a search for an appropriate uncertainty variable is that of incomplete knowledge. If we do not have an exhaustive list of mutually exclusive alternatives, then we cannot use a distributed variable, and so we must consider a non-distributional measure. Shackle (1961) put forward the idea of *potential surprise* as such a measure.

As we have already mentioned, when we assign probabilities to a set of outcomes we are assuming a finite and exhaustive list of possibilities. When we say that a thing is possible we mean that it is accepted as an item on this list; conversely if we assert that something is impossible we mean that it is not accepted as an item on the list. The latter statement implies a precise probability for that item, *viz.* that it is zero. The former statement is much less precise; it simply implies that the probability assigned to that item will be non-zero. This does not, however, exhaust the meanings of the word 'possible' in common usage. We may refer to a future event as being 'perfectly possible'; by this we mean that we feel that it is likely; or to put it another way, we would not be surprised if it happened. However we are not simply using 'possible' as a synonym for 'probable'. Several alternative states of affairs may seem to me to be 'perfectly possible' or 'scarcely possible' and the probability of each one, in the distributional sense, *must* be related to the number of alternative states I am prepared to consider. The addition or deletion of one or several states from my list may not, however, alter the degree of possibility which I am prepared to assign to each individual statement[2]. By this criterion, possibility is non-distributional.

We take possibility in this context to mean "consonant, to a greater or lesser extent, with the decision-maker's conception of the nature of the world and its immediate state" (Shackle, 1961, p. 76). Shackle then suggests that *potential surprise* is the expression, in terms of feeling, of degrees of possibility, and that potential surprise could be used as a non-distributional uncertainty variable. If we assign the value of zero potential surprise when possibility is at a maximum, the non-distributional character of this variable becomes obvious, since it would then be meaningless to add together the degrees of potential surprise assigned to an exhaustive set of rival hypotheses regarding the total (zero) so obtained as being distributed over the alternatives. (Unless that is, with great perversity, all non-zero numbers are given a negative sign! The introduction of a concept of negative potential surprise seems unlikely to elucidate our argument.)

Zero potential surprise, then, corresponds to perfect possibility in

Shackle's thesis. Consequently if we say that two rival hypotheses are perfectly possible we are also saying that they are *equally* possible, for either will occasion zero surprise if it proves true. Furthermore there is no limit to the number of rival hypotheses which may simultaneously accord zero surprise, and so situations can be accommodated which pose difficulties for a distributional variable. For example a person may wish to give equal status to an hypothesis *A* and its contradiction *not-A*, say, 'it will rain today' and 'it will not rain today'. With a distributional probability variable, this must result in a probability of one-half being assigned to the two alternatives. Now *not-A* is clearly capable of subdivision into several other rival hypotheses, for instance: (a) it will snow, (b) it will be sunny, (c) it will do something else (the residual hypothesis). With potential surprise as a variable there is no difficulty in assigning equal status to some or all of these rivals, but with the distributional variable I cannot assign equal status to *A*, *not-A*, *and* the subdivision of *not-A* all at the same time because the probabilities assigned to the subdivision of *not-A* must sum to the probability assigned to *not-A*.

Shackle has formalized the ideas of potential surprise into a set of axioms (Shackle, 1961; pp. 80–85) and it is clear from them that the notions of possibility and potential surprise give us far more freedom to make assumptions about the psychological processes which result in decisions and choices than do the axioms of probability theory, which demand basically additive or multiplicative processes only. For example let us consider, from both standpoints, an instance in which the joint (simultaneous) truth of two independent (non-rival) hypotheses is in question. Using the usual axioms of probability we find that the probability of the two hypotheses being simultaneously true is the product of their independent probabilities. By the usual actuarial means it has been determined that the probability of someone having blood group O is roughly 0.4 and the probability of a person having blood group Rhesus negative is 0.15. Thus the probability of finding someone with O Rhesus negative blood is 0.06, and this indeed reflects the proportion of such a combination which I would expect to find in a large sample. But what about the particular case? Using Shackle's axioms we find a rather different answer. He would predict that my surprise is no greater than the greater of

[the surprise that I have at finding a person with blood group O] and

> [the surprise I have at finding an individual with blood group Rhesus negative *given that* I am not surprised at finding an individual with blood group O][3].

So if I am not surprised by finding someone with blood group O (as seems reasonable) then the first proposition has zero surprise value, and the second one has some higher surprise value. So my surprise at the combination of characteristics is no greater than the surprise at finding someone with Rhesus negative blood, and hence is dependent on this feature alone. Similarly, consider the combination of black hair and violet-coloured eyes as against brown hair and violet-coloured eyes. Without bothering with the exact figures we conclude from probability calculations that since brown hair is more common than black hair, the former combination, being rarer, should be the more startling when it is observed. On Shackle's axioms, however, given that both black and brown hair engender zero surprise (again, as seems reasonable) the two combinations engender *equal* surprise which is due entirely to the unusual eye colour. This seems a more realistic conclusion than that which would have been reached from probability considerations.

CONSEQUENCES

Although the examples used in the preceding section are trivial, they do illustrate some of the features of a non-distributional uncertainty variable in contrast with conventional probability, and we have argued in favour of the former as being more appropriate in many situations. What then are the implications of these arguments for the study of human behaviour? The clearest area of application is in studying the general problem of decision-making. A review of this area is beyond the scope of this essay, but Shackle has developed his ideas into a theory of economic decision-making which is quite different from the games-of-chance type of model originated by von Neuman and Morgenstern (1955) held by some to have wrought disaster upon economic theories. As far as we are aware this model has not been tested in the context of less specialized behaviour, but the possibilities are clearly great, and the empirical difficulties by no means insuperable. It should be quite feasible, for instance, to apply some of the methods used by Cohen (1964) to study simple situations.

Some areas of psychological research, whilst less obviously concerned with decision-making, may require subjects in experiments to make implicit decisions before emitting the behaviour which comprises the data of such studies. An interesting example of this genre are the phenomena known collectively as *attribution process*. This term refers to the ways in which people attribute to others intentions, and characteristics, on the basis of what they observe. It has been found that, on the whole, when faced with qualitatively conflicting information about another person an individual will be most likely to concentrate on one kind (say, that which is pleasant) at the expense of the rest, or to invent some possible explanation which resolves the conflict (Hastorf, Schneider and Polefka, 1970). No explanation for these 'styles' of attribution (known respectively as the discounting and relational modes) has been found, but they clearly have features in common with the ideas which we have developed. In the first place a consequence of Shackle's axioms is that if some hypothesis generates zero surprise, then when this occurs in combination with another hypothesis which generates non-zero surprise, attention is focused on that latter hypothesis. In other words, to return to attribution processes, there is a basis for prediction or behaviour in the discounting mode given information about the potential surprise of the material presented to subjects. Secondly there is clearly scope for investigation into the basis of 'possible explanations' devised by subjects who try to bring together apparently contradictory information in the relational mode. We may ask, for example, whether people prefer to use all the information at their disposal, and use the discounting mode only if they are unable to invent an adequate 'possible explanation'. If so, a wealth of data would be forthcoming from a study of how such explanations are derived, and what constitutes the criterion of possiblity[4].

Finally, we should consider whether there are any implications of this line of thought for the behaviour of undertaking research and, for that matter, writing essays about it! Little has been written about the behaviour of research workers, and so we offer one speculation. The decision as to whether the data from a particular experiment do or do not support the experimenter's hypothesis is usually, and properly, made using statistical tests. If the test proves negative it is necessary to 'accept the null hypothesis'. That is to say accept that the data were not influenced by the experimental conditions; and that should be the end of the matter. Yet is is noticeable that scientists do not, in practice, work that way, although one would think so to read published accounts of their work. In truth we (and the author must include himself) may well feel that there is a *distinct possibility* that our ideas are correct, experimental evidence notwithstanding, and our efforts are directed by that judgment and not the formal statistical criteria. This dual level of decision-making, if it exists, is not simply extra evidence for the worth of the ideas we have tried to explain; it is one of the sustaining influences on scientific endeavour.

ACKNOWLEDGMENT

The author is most grateful to Mrs B. Morris for secretarial assistance.

NOTES

1. The issue here may have become more confused by the use of the common distinction between 'objective' and 'subjective' probabilities. We might more properly refer to 'empirical' and (say) 'intuitive' probabilities to distinguish estimates made on the basis of systematic and repeatable observations from those which are not.

2. There is a superficial resemblance between this idea and the notion of probability as 'degrees of belief' (Augustus de Morgan, 1847). The resemblance *is* superficial, however, because proponents of that view hold that the complement of the degree of belief in an hypothesis is a measure of the degree of disbelief in the same hypothesis. This means, implicitly, that degrees of belief are of a distributional nature.

3. In formal terms this axiom is stated as follows: "Let Y_A^B be the degree of potential surprise assigned to hypothesis *B* when Y^A is the degree assigned to hypothesis *A*, and let Y_B^0 be the degree assigned to *B* when $Y^A = 0$. Then Y_A^B is not greater than the greater of Y^A, Y_0^B" (Shackle, 1961; p. 80).

4. There is, of course, one further mode of attribution under these circumstances; that is where people give weights to positive and negative information and make a final attribution on the basis of some weighted average. It is purported to be the least common mode (Hastorf, Schneider and Polefka, 1970) and does not clearly relate to our topic.

BIBLIOGRAPHY

Bernoulli, J. (1713). *Ars Conjectandi*. Basileae: impensis Thurnisiorum fratrum (Basle: Thurn Brothers)

Broadbent, D. E. (1958). *Perception and Communication*. (Oxford: Pergamon Press)

Cattell, R. B. (1957). *Personality and Motivation: Structure and Measurement*. (New York: World Books)

Cohen, J. (1964). *Behaviour in Uncertainty*. (London: Allen and Unwin)

Cohen, J. and Christensen, I. P. (1970). *Information and Choice*. (Edinburgh: Oliver and Boyd)

Hastorf, A. H., Schneider, D. J. and Polefka, J. (1970). *Person Perception*. (Reading, Mass.: Addison-Wesley)

Meredith, P. (1964). Models, Meanings and Men. In J. Cohen (ed.) *Readings in Psychology*. (London: Allen and Unwin)

de Morgan, A. (1847). *Formal Logic*. (London: Taylor and Walton)

von Neuman, J. and Morgenstern, O. (1955). *Theory of Games and Economic Behaviour*. (Princeton University Press)

Shackle, G. L. S. (1961). *Decision, Order and Time in Human Affairs*. (Cambridge University Press)

Spearman, C. (1927). *The Abilities of Man*. (New York: Basic Books)

4

The Perception of Probability

VIOLET R. CANE and
PETER O. GOLDBLATT

Those who set out to base a theory of statistical inference on personal (or subjective) probability – the Bayesian approach – assume that there is an idealized sort of person described as 'rational' or 'coherent' who can assign probabilities to events in such a way that they satisfy the mathematical axioms of probability. The probability value which such a person associates with a particular event can, it is supposed, be extracted from him by confronting him with a succession of choices, ever more refined, which are designed to pin down this value as exactly as is required. Psychologists conducting experiments with ordinary human beings, however, find that they do not behave like the 'rational' person; the choices they make, or the probabilities they state, do not for example agree with such probability laws as the addition and multiplication rules.

There are two ways of reacting to the demonstrated difference between the ideal person and real people; one is to say that people are wrong and should be taught to be coherent and consistent; the other is to see whether observed behaviour under uncertainty has its own rules, capable of precise or at least statistical description. The contrast is rather like that between, on the one hand, a learning theorist wedded to some strict model of learning, who demonstrates by very constrained experiments that animals do in fact learn in accordance with his model, and, on the other hand, an ethologist prepared to investigate the behaviour of animals in their natural environments. In the imaginary experiments which are to determine the rational person's probabilities it is, for instance, assumed that his idea of the probability attaching to a given event is not only exact but stable; so that successive questions refer in fact to the same numerical probability value. However it would seem reasonable to suppose that the perception of a probability value is at least as fluctuating and inexact as the perception of the intensity of a light, in fact that all the problems that arise in psychophysics, of defining thresholds, dealing with order effects and so on, would equally arise in this case.

THE DERIVATION OF PERCEPTUAL LAWS

If we consider the experiments of the German school of psychologists in the nineteenth century which led to the formulation of the Weber-Fechner law, we see that a necessary preliminary to these was that the stimuli used should be measurable by a physical process. Such a way of measuring must however have been based on direct perception. In the case of weight, for example, there must be agreement that some objects are heavier than some others; given a series of objects grossly different in weight, there must be consensus about their rank order by weight, irrespective of size. Rational discussion must then lead to the idea that two bricks weigh twice as much as one brick, so that it is possible to establish a scale for weight of, at any rate, a crude sort. The use of a balance with an arm carrying a movable weight converts this crude scale into a measurement of length, and enables any object to be assigned a weight to a certain degree of accuracy. Other measures of stimulus intensity, for instance temperature, amount of light or sound, are obtained in a similar way: that is they are based on the rank order of perceived differences and an agreed way of formulating a linear scale. If a more refined method of measurement is invented it agrees with the existing form of measurement wherever gross differences are involved and deals with smaller differences by linear interpolation. What Weber's Law says then (and we take this law to be a reasonable approximation to the facts) is that, in terms of intensities measured on a rational scale, the perceptual system works with ratios; if we wish to think of it as working with differences like a physical scale then, as Fechner pointed out, we have to suppose that the perceptual system perceives the logarithm of a physically measured intensity.

What does this suggest about the perception of probability? First, we have to assume that human beings can assign probabilities to the occurrence of alternative events, but since, like most living organisms, they can choose between actions in situations of uncertainty and can modify their choice in the light of experience this assumption does not seem unreasonable. Moreover a certain uniformity in the results of learning experiments suggests that there is some agreement about probability values. (We may also note that committees sometimes agree on a choice between actions; the situation in this case is more complicated since the various members of the committee may be using different pay-off matrices.) A way of measuring probability, agreed among mathematicians, is already available. The probability that an event A will occur is a real number, p, lying between 0 and 1; values of p near 1 mean that the event is very likely to occur, values near 0 that it is most unlikely to occur; the extreme values 0, 1 mean that non-occurrence and occurrence, respectively, are certain for all practical purposes. If we wished to check that such a scale corresponded with ordinary feelings about probability it would be sensible to do it by means of an urn model. We should need to persuade our subjects that what is going to happen can be represented by drawing a ball from a well-shaken urn containing red and white balls of identical size and texture. Drawing a red ball would represent that the event A occurred, drawing a white ball would represent that it did not. The extreme cases – all balls red or all balls white – would appear to present no difficulty; but does the case where half the balls are red accurately represent the feeling that nothing can be said either way? Does a high proportion of red balls represent the idea that the event is very likely to occur? People who are taught probability generally come to accept this representation of probability as reasonable; perhaps we can regard this as agreement enough.

One difficulty about comparing the probability scale with scales used for measuring other types of stimuli is that it is bounded above as well as below. It is therefore more convenient to use a related scale, the odds ratio or odds in favour of the event, $p/(1-p)$; since this is used in betting, and is apparently widely understood, it is possible that it represents more closely our sensations in trying to estimate a probability – we weigh occurrence against non-occurrence and in particular regard equal weights as representing equal likelihood. Such a scale runs from zero to infinity, like those for measuring light intensity or weight. By analogy with results for those modalities we might therefore expect that the perceptual scale for which threshold differences were constant would be $\log p - \log(1-p)$.

Thus for some specified stimulus I a just noticeably different stimulus I' would satisfy the relation $| I - I' | = k I$ where k is constant for a given subject and conditions of observation; since $I = p / (1 - p)$, $I' = p' / (1 - p')$, it follows that $| p - p' | = k p (1 - p)$ which is greatest when $p = \frac{1}{2}$. Thus comparison of probabilities which are close together should be most difficult when both are near $\frac{1}{2}$. However, again by analogy with the perception of light, Weber's Law should break down when I is near 0 or very large, and the existence of an absolute threshold would suggest that probabilities smaller than some value c would be indistinguishable from each other and from 0, with a similar result near $p = 1$. One would expect in fact that a probability of c or less would be treated as 0 but described as c if the occurrence of the corresponding event could clearly not be regarded as impossible. There is some slight evidence for this in Cohen, Chesnick and Haran (1972); subjects required to assign probabilities to events whose computed probabilities were of the order of 10^{-3} rarely used values less than 0.1.

FLUCTUATIONS IN PERCEPTION

It is not of course correct to talk about the absolute threshold as a constant, as we did in the preceding section. Stimuli within threshold distance of each other are not in general treated as equal, more often they are differentiated but not in a consistent way; if I and I' are compared repeatedly and I' is sometimes thought to be greater than I and sometimes less then what is to be called a threshold can only be settled statistically. Usually I' is said to be just noticeably greater than I if in repeated comparisons made by one subject it is described as greater on some fixed percentage (say 80%) of occasions. If such fluctuations occur in the perception of probability then any attempt to pinpoint a value of a personal probability by auxiliary questions or a succession of gambles would merely lead to inconsistency and confusion.

There appears to be indirect evidence for such fluctuation in an experiment described by Cohen and Chesnick (1970) which essentially sets out to determine subjective probabilities by the limiting method. A simple case of a limiting method experiment is as follows: a subject is asked to compare a stimulus of strength $2\frac{1}{2}$ with each of four other stimuli of strengths 1, 2, 3 and 4 respectively, either by an upward run or by a downward run. In an upward run he first compares 1 with $2\frac{1}{2}$ and if he says 1 is smaller he then compares 2 with $2\frac{1}{2}$ and so on; the run stops when he first comes to a stimulus which he says is greater than $2\frac{1}{2}$. A downward run is performed similarly but starting with 4 and stopping with the first stimulus said to be less than $2\frac{1}{2}$. If in an upward run 2 is said to be greater than $2\frac{1}{2}$ then 3 and 4 are not tested, but it is assumed that they would be perceived as greater than $2\frac{1}{2}$. However the subject's perceptions may fluctuate so rapidly that successive comparisons can be taken as independent and 3 (or 4) might be observed as less than $2\frac{1}{2}$. Suppose we had data from repeated comparisons made by the same subject of 1 with $2\frac{1}{2}$, 2 with $2\frac{1}{2}$ and so on and that the proportion of times that 1, 2, 3, 4 respectively were judged greater than $2\frac{1}{2}$ was $0, \frac{1}{3}, \frac{2}{3}, 1$; then for upward runs, assuming rapid perceptual fluctuations, the proportion of runs in which the stopping point was 1, 2, 3, 4 would be $0, \frac{1}{3}, \frac{4}{9}, \frac{2}{9}$ (the result for 3, for example, is calculated from the fact that it would only be tested on two-thirds of the runs and on two-thirds of the test occasions would be judged greater). If we forgot about the possibility of fluctuations we should calculate that the proportion of times 1, 2, 3, 4 was preferred to $2\frac{1}{2}$ was $0, \frac{1}{3}, \frac{1}{3}+\frac{4}{9}, \frac{1}{3}+\frac{4}{9}+\frac{2}{9}$ or that the preference for $2\frac{1}{2}$ was $1, \frac{2}{3}, \frac{2}{9}, 0$. Similar calculations with downward runs would give that the preference for $2\frac{1}{2}$ over 1, 2, 3, 4 was $1, \frac{7}{9}, \frac{1}{3}, 0$. These are not the same results; there is a kind of hysteresis effect, with the preference graph for the downward runs lying above that for the upward runs. Cohen and Chesnick's experiment is much more complicated than this, but a simulation which takes account of the experimental details produces the same sort of results, which are in fact a characteristic of the limiting method when independent fluctuations of perception occur rapidly – see Brown and Cane (1959). Cohen and Chesnick used different subjects and not repeated runs with the same subject, so we have to assume that they all (with the exception of the 40% who worked out the problem mathematically) had much the same perception of probability and much the same rate of fluctuation.

SOME RECENT EXPERIMENTS

We have been carrying out some experiments relating to the three questions that were discussed earlier:

(i) does a person show consistency in his judgment of probability and in particular does he show consistency when the conditions are varied in ways which should be irrelevant;
(ii) if so, do the judgments of different people agree;
(iii) if so, do the results agree with probabilities calculated mathematically?

We wanted to ask for estimates of probability values because we were also interested in the sort of scales that were used, so we took as subjects university students who had just finished the first year of a mathematics course; these students had had a few lectures in probability theory and would at least understand what we were asking. Such subjects could not be confronted with a lottery problem because the mathematical probabilities are too easy to calculate and would very likely be used; in any case, we felt it would be better to require the abstraction of a probability from a physical situation. We decided to use a version of shove-ha'penny; that is, an object was to be tossed on to a table top divided into a regular network of cells and the subject was to be asked to estimate the probabilities that it would fall entirely within one cell or overlap a number of cells in various ways. The type of object and of network could be varied easily and so could the scale of the network.

We used three basic arrangements:

(a) a disc thrown on a network of squares;
(b) a disc thrown on a network of diamonds of given angle;
(c) a needle thrown on a network of squares (Buffon's needle).

In cases (a) and (b) the ratio of the diameter of the disc to the perpendicular distance between opposite sides of the cell was 0.3, 0.5 or 0.7 and disc diameters of 1.5, 2.2, and 3.6 cm were used, so that taking all possible combinations there were nine experimental conditions for each case. Similarly there were nine experimental conditions for case (c) although different ratios (0.5, 0.7, 1.0) were used. Twenty-seven students did twenty-seven trials each (all conditions) according to a balanced design. Given the shape of the object and of the cell the calculated probabilities depend only on the ratio, so that each subject was in theory repeating each estimation problem three times.

Real discs, table tops and tosses were used but the fall of the object was not visible to the subject. However subjects were shown the network and allowed to handle the object before each trial. Subjects were asked to estimate the probabilities p_1, p_3, p_4 that the object would fall entirely within one cell, would overlap exactly three cells, or would overlap exactly four cells, respectively. We did not ask about the remaining possibility, that it would overlap two cells, because we did not want subjects to try to make probabilities add to one. (In fact, the probabilities they estimated for the three cases sometimes summed to more than one.) On each trial they were also asked to choose a 'best bet', and on some trials were given a prize if the object fell according to their choice.

For the disc/square combination, ratio 0.3, the calculated probabilities p_1, p_3, p_4 are 0.490, 0.019, 0.071. Of the 81 responses, 78 gave p_1 as greatest, 48 of these ordered the other two correctly and 10 gave them equal values; there was thus considerable agreement both within and between subjects. For the ratio 0.5, for which p_1, p_3, p_4 are 0.250, 0.054, 0.196, the results were almost as good, for the ratio 0.7, for which p_1, p_3, p_4 are 0.090, 0.105, 0.385 the results were less good, even allowing for ties for the two lowest probabilities. Among the 27 subjects, 13 were self-consistent and 10 of these gave the theoretical rank order. The disc/diamond combination, for which the calculated probabilities are:

Ratio	0.3	0.5	0.7
p_1	0.490	0.250	0.090
p_3	0.055	0.152	0.298
p_4	0.035	0.098	0.192

was obviously found more difficult, especially for the ratio 0.7; here 11 were self-consistent but only 6 of them agreed with the calculated probability order. Self-consistency appears to be a property of the subject – of the 13 who were self-consistent for the square, 8 were self-consistent for the diamond; however only 1 was both self-consistent and correct in both cases. Even the self-consistent subjects gave very variable estimates of the probabilities, so it is to be assumed that they were not performing mathematical calculations.

The replies in the needle/square case were surprisingly accurate; it was in a way simpler because the needle could not lie in four cells, so that p_4 was 0 always. We asked the subjects for an estimate of p_4 so as to see whether they were thinking about the problem or just guessing; very few mistakes were made and then only in the earlier trials.

The experimental results have not yet been completely analysed and we hope to get interesting information about the numerical values people use to describe probabilities, since this may throw light on the threshold problem and on whether the odds ratio is a natural measurement.

In conclusion we should like to stress how valuable we have found John Cohen's work in the area of subjective probability, in its general approach as much as in its detail. Almost all human, and indeed animal, behaviour is based on ideas or fears about the future and consequently on the evaluation of the chances of future events; the study of subjective probability must always lie at the centre of psychological research.

BIBLIOGRAPHY

Brown, J. and Cane, V. R. (1959), An analysis of the limiting method. *British Journal of Statistical Psychology*, **12,** 119–126

Cohen, J. and Chesnick, E. I. (1970). The doctrine of psychological chances. *British Journal of Psychology*, **61,** 323–334

Cohen, J., Chesnick, E. I. and Haran, D. (1972). A confirmation of the inertial-ψ effect in sequential choice and decision. *British Journal of Psychology*, **63,** 41–46

5

Paradoxes in Uncertainty and Coincidence

C. E. M. HANSEL

A difficulty arising in the study of subjective probability is that a number of words such as 'expectation', 'confidence', and 'subjective probability' itself are employed in more than one way.

The position is similar to that arising in the study of sensory processes where inadequacy of definition has led to confusion owing to the use of terms such as 'heaviness', 'brightness' and 'loudness' to describe the objective stimuli that evoke these subjective qualities.

After about 100 years of experimental research the relationship between brightness, radiant energy and luminance is becoming clear, but misunderstandings still arise through the use of words that denote the magnitude of a subjective factor such as a sensation, to describe the stimulus that is responsible for evoking it.

The term Subjective Probability is being employed here as it was used by John Cohen in the early 1950s in connection with gambling and risk-taking. It was at that time realized that decisions a person makes in a particular situation may be dependent on his personal expectation of being successful or on his idea of the risk involved, rather than on any *a priori* probability that might be assigned to his being successful or not. A person familiar with the determination of probabilities may in some circumstances estimate the probability of an event, and this estimate may influence his subjective probability regarding the event. The two may not be identical or even similar since a man may realize that the odds are loaded against a particular horse winning a race but he may still have an overwhelming feeling that he is going to back a winner.

Subjective probability in this sense, as a measure of expectation, may be assigned a magnitude. Thus a subject may consider two possible events and decide whether he considers one of them more likely, less likely, or equally likely to arise than the other; a value may be assigned on a magnitude scale, or a person familiar with the concept of 'odds' may relate his state of expectation to a well-understood probability measure – say, odds of 1 in 10. If subjective probability is represented by values between 0 and 1 on a scale, the value 1 represents certainty that an outcome will arise, or that it will not arise; i.e. the subjective probability of performing a clearly impossible task, say, jumping over the moon, will not be zero, but the subjective probability of not clearing it will be 1. A state of surprise may arise, following a state of certainty regarding an event, if the outcome does not conform to expectation. Subjective probability may indicate a measure of expectation regarding a future event or be retrospective. Thus, following awareness of an event, a person may be surprised if it is one to which he would have assigned a subjective probability of 1 of it not arising.

EXPECTATIONS

It may be expected that during the individual's development some correspondence will arise between expectations and observed events, in the same manner that stability is achieved in perception. In the study of perceptual phenomena a major source of information leading to the development of theory has been the study of phenomena that are at a variance with a person's expectations. The aim here is to consider similar phenomena arising in a person's expectations about events and causality, since these may indicate the manner in which an individual's states of mind and behaviour are dependent on factors arising during development and knowledge of causal relationships.

The cases considered here are of two types: the first arising in sophisticated individuals in their understanding of processes in which there is an element of indeterminism; the second with the Monte-Carlo effect in which expectations appear to be inconsistent with, and to override knowledge about, the nature of random events.

Paradoxical situations, of the first type, have been highlighted by Koestler (Hardy, Harvie and Koestler, 1973). These he considers indicate 'quirks' in probability theory and the nature of coincidence.

These will first be considered as cases where expectations are at variance with predictions from probability theory and the understanding normally achieved through the observation of natural events.

COINCIDENCES

Koestler is primarily concerned with explaining extraordinary coincidences that arise in everyday life, such as those collected within parapsychology, that are difficult to account for in terms of chance occurrence. Accepting the fact that such cases are frequently reported, and providing a fresh crop of such cases from his own correspondence he suggests that these indicate a common 'acausal principle' operating in nature, which is responsible for coincidences and simultaneous thoughts. This principle he suggests can also account for a number of paradoxical phenomena in probability theory. Whether it is necessary to invoke any new principle or not, it is clear that Koestler has collected together instances where he finds disagreement between subjective and objective probabilities, and that similar disagreements are found by a large part of the population.

Koestler's first paradox arises in seeking to reconcile indeterminacy of isolated events with the orderly properties that are present with large numbers of such events. After considering examples where order appears to emerge in this manner, he concludes that

> there is a basic flaw or inadequacy in the current concepts of chance and randomness, which calls for some additional hypothesis to account for the spontaneous emergence of order from disorder. . . .

His first case concerns events at the level of quantum physics. He writes

> . . . the point in time at which a radioactive atom will disintegrate is totally unpredictable . . . and yet it does have a hidden relationship with the rest of the world because the 'half-life period' of any grain of a radio-active substance . . . is precisely fixed and predictable. . . . There are fluctuations: somewhere

> along the road, there may be an excess of deceased atoms over the predicted mean, or a deficit. But it will soon be put right. How is this done, since the individual disintegrations are uncaused and physically uninfluenced by what goes on in the rest of the grain?

Harvie, one of Koestler's co-authors, makes a similar point. He writes:

> . . . although in a collection of, say, one million nuclei of the same kind, it is impossible to say exactly when any one of them will disintegrate, we know that after a time equivalent to the half-life only half a million will survive unchanged (p. 129).

Koestler provides other instances where large numbers of unpredictable events can lead to more or less predictable averages. The first is concerned with the average numbers of reports of dogs biting people each day in New York, the second with the numbers of people murdered in each 10-year period in England and Wales, and the third with the numbers of cavalry horses administering fatal kicks to soldiers in the German Army of the last century.

Considering data from the New York City Department of Health, he notes that the average number of reports per day of dogs biting people remained at a relatively stable value being: in 1955 – 75.3; in 1956 – 73.6; in 1957 – 73.5; in 1958 – 74.5; and in 1959 – 72.4.

He observes a similar consistency in figures for average murders per million of the population over 10-year periods from 1920 to 1969, and also in the numbers of cavalry horses administering fatal kicks to soldiers. He remarks that:

> cavalry horses administering fatal kicks to soldiers in the German Army of the last century . . . were apparently guided by the so-called Poisson equation of probability theory.

Here he is presumably referring to data discussed by Fisher (1946) in his *Statistical Methods for Research Workers*. There Fisher gives figures originally obtained by Bortkewitch from the records of ten army corps over a period of 20 years. The number of deaths arising in each of 200 samples was noted. The observed frequencies, when compared with theoretical figures based on the Poisson distribution, gave a remarkably close fit.

Koestler concludes:

> How do the dogs of New York know when to stop biting, and when to make up the daily quota? How do the murderers of England and Wales know to stop at four victims per million? It may seem that I am labouring the point, but this question is indeed at the centre of the whole problem of chance and design. Since the chains of events that led to each individual murder, or atomic decay, are ostensibly unconnected with each other, we must assume that the fulfilment of the statistical prediction is itself due to blind coincidence, or else we are driven to opt for some alternative hypothesis on the lines discussed in previous sections, such as Jung-Pauli's acausal connecting principle or the convergence effect.

Considering first the case concerning radioactive decay, difficulty arises in the use of the term 'precisely'. If the grain of radioactive material consisted of one atom it would have no half-life period, and according to his definition neither could any odd number of atoms. The half-life period becomes specifiable in terms of a mean and standard deviation as the number of atoms constituting the grain increases. It can never be numerically precise in view of the indeterminate behaviour of single atoms. Harvie's half-million constitutes the most likely number of atoms to survive, but it is unlikely that exactly that number will survive in a particular sample just as it becomes increasingly unlikely as the number of pennies tossed is increased that exactly half will turn up heads. Again putting the question the other way round it may be asked, what is the probability after precisely time t seconds that half the number of atoms will have disintegrated? This is equivalent to asking the question: what is the probability that a man randomly selected from a population will be precisely 6 feet tall? It is a meaningless question, or at the most would be answered by saying that it would be zero since the number of categories of exact height into which the population could be divided would be infinite. It is more likely that tossing two pennies will result in exactly one head and one tail than that tossing 100 pennies will result in 50 heads and 50 tails. In general at the macro-level the end-state is less determinable than at the micro-level.

SAMPLES

It may be asked whether subjective estimates about the numbers of events of a particular category in different-sized samples of random events conform to expectations on the basis of probability theory or whether they show marked deviations.

Some answers may be found in experiments carried out with 12-year-old children (Cohen and Hansel, 1956). The children were shown an urn containing approximately equal numbers of blue and yellow beads. They saw a sample of four drawn at random and placed without revealing their identities in a beaker. This process was repeated until 16 sets of 4 beads had been placed in separate beakers. The subject had to guess the number of beakers – without specifying particular beakers – containing 0, 1, 2, 3 and 4 blue (or yellow) beads. The predictions were not unlike those predicted from theory either in terms of an urn containing equal numbers of blue and yellow beads or in terms of the binomial expansion calculated from the total numbers of red and green beads allocated by each subject.

The replies of individual children indicated that they regarded 2 blue and 2 yellow beads as more likely to arise than 1 blue and 3 yellow or vice versa and then 4 blue and 4 yellow.

The cases cited by Koestler in connection with dogs, horses, and murderers are all consistent with what would be expected if the data were obtained by random sampling from a fixed population. Here again, however, Koestler discusses the behaviour of individual dogs, horses and murderers, whereas he presents average values for the populations concerned. If he had presented his data in the form of the actual numbers of events arising during the various time-periods the variations present are hardly likely to have puzzled many people, whether statistically sophisticated or not. Thus the values for dogs biting people (multiply the averages by 365) were in 1955 – 27 484; in 1956 – 26 864; in 1957 – 26 827; in 1958 – 27 192; and in 1959 – 26 426. It might then have been asked why 1058 more bites were administered in 1959 than in 1955, and possibly some cause – such as a hot summer or an outbreak of rabies – might have been sought to account for the difference. This type of paradox, as with that of radioactive decay times, appears to arise when considering derived values – i.e. ratios and averages rather than discrete events – and then treating these as if they constituted events.

There remains the problem underlying Koestler's discussion of remarkable coincidences in everyday life, that seem to imply some connection or causal basis. Accounts of such happenings have been reported for the past hundred years in psychical research in the attempt to provide evidence for life after death, telepathy and other paranormal phenomena. The conclusions drawn from them are no different today than they were a century ago. It is remarkable, however, that in any audience of intelligent individuals, familiar with findings in the study of testimony, perception and memory, a number are likely to be present who report having private experiences or familiarity with particular cases which nevertheless they find inexplicable.

TEMPORAL 'CONTIGUITY' AND CAUSALITY

Considering the multiplicity of events arising continuously in the individual's environment in natural conditions, it is apparent that under normal circumstances juxtaposition in time of disconnected events does not itself attract attention, but in certain cases the contiguity of two *perceived* events may lead to the assumption of a causal relationship. The important feature is the time relationship between perceiving the events.

In accounts of the type discussed by Koestler the time dimension is important both when considering the degree of coincidence and in relation to psychological factors affecting the accuracy of the account. Thus the individual providing the account has a particular experience usually of a striking nature, and later learns about the second event which has occurred at some distant location. Or, after observing an event he recalls an experience he had in the past. Puzzlement, therefore, arises in retrospect when attempting to reconcile the occurrence of the seemingly independent events.

Most of the accounts are produced a considerable time, often years, after the events. Thus both recollection of the events and of the time interval separating them is likely to change, and also to undergo modifications at each recounting or recall of the event, so that it becomes more remarkable with the passage of time.

One of the small number of accounts where it was later possible to check back and find the precise time at which two coincident events happened was reported in 1883 after careful investigation by two investigators (Gurney and Myers, 1884). It was recounted by Sir Edmond Hornby, formerly Chief Judge of the Consular Court at Shanghai, and concerned an event that took place *9 years earlier*. The coincidence arose because a reporter burst into the Judge's bedroom at 1.30 a.m. to ask about a decision he was to make the following day. The appearance of the reporter, and the time of the event, were vouched for by Lady Hornby who was in bed with her husband when the reporter burst into the room. On going to court next day Judge Hornby heard that the reporter had not left his house that night but had been found dead in bed by his wife at 1.30 a.m.

Later check on public records revealed that the reporter had died between 8 and 9 a.m. (Balfour, 1884). It also transpired that there was no official record of the case on which the story hinged, and, incidentally, that Judge Hornby was not married until 3 months after the date of the reporter's death.

The judge, when confronted with these facts, could only say that his vision must have followed the death instead of synchronizing with it.

A particular case in which expectations appear to be at variance with observations of past events arises in the Monte-Carlo effect, in which a gambler's certainty that a particular outcome will arise increases as the length of the run of the alternate outcome increases. Here gamblers who are attempting to predict random events over very large numbers of trials, with knowledge of results after each trial and monetary reinforcement following successful prediction, have expectations that are inconsistent with theory and observation.

Experiments with children and adults have indicated that the Monte-Carlo effect is present at an early age, and becomes modified with experience. Thus when predicting the next outcome in a series of random binary events young children tended to alternate between the two outcomes, older children alternated in the main with some repetitions but gave no longer sequences, whereas adults produced series more similar to a random series but showing a tendency to favour a change in the outcome thus displaying the Monte-Carlo effect (Cohen and Hansel, 1956).

The types of sequence encountered in everyday life (other than in the gaming rooms through random sampling) are, however, seldom random. A child who tends to favour a non-preponderant outcome is predicting in a manner that is no less effective than any other manner for a random sequence in producing correct predictions, and which will be effective in the type of sequence represented by taking successive samples without replacement that often arises in everyday life. It is thus an effective method of prediction when the nature of the series is unknown. In addition where the time element is of importance it will provide clear advantages. Thus the child predicting random binary outcomes, who alternates from the one outcome to the other, will provide more correct predictions, in a given length of time, than one who is in a state of uncertainty.

It has also been found (Cohen and Hansel, 1956) that while the Monte-Carlo effect may be evident when predicting an event arising in a series of outcomes it does not affect the manner in which successive samples provide evidence about the nature of the population from which they are drawn. Thus, groups of children and adults were confronted with an urn which they were told contained a mixture of 100 blue and yellow beads. A bead was then extracted from the urn and, before its identity was revealed, half the members of each group had to predict its colour and the other half the number of blue beads in the urn. They were then shown the bead which was then replaced in the urn. The process was repeated until 20 beads had been seen.

It was found that the predictions of the contents of the urn given by both children and adults tended to be dependent on the relative numbers of blue and yellow beads withdrawn, but the group having to predict the colour drawn, after seeing a run of a particular colour, tended to favour to an increasing extent the alternative colour. This was particularly evident in the children and to a lesser extent in the adults.

In addition it was found, particularly with the children, that estimates tended to be influenced more by recent outcomes than by those occurring earlier in the series. This again is an appropriate way to respond to a series where the relative proportions in which the events arise are changing systematically.

Thus if a series consists of two types of event arising in different proportions, the most effective initial strategy might be to predict in terms of the relative numbers of each event that have occurred. If, however, the proportions are changing systematically over time periods such a system would be non-adaptive. By taking into account more recent events the system can adjust itself to such changes. Adaptive processes and learning, which are time-dependent, afford a means whereby such averaging can arise, through the weight given to past events diminishing with the passage of time or after modifications by more recent events, thus enabling particular characteristics to establish themselves and at the same time also enabling the system to cope with slow overall changes.

BIBLIOGRAPHY

Balfour, F. H. (1884). Letter. *Nineteenth Century* (November), **16**

Cohen, J. and Hansel, C. E. M. (1956). *Risk and Gambling*. (New York: Longmans)

Fisher, R. A. (1946). *Statistical Methods for Research Workers* (10th edn.). (Edinburgh: Oliver and Boyd)

Gurney, E. and Myers, F. W. H. (1884). Visible apparitions. *Nineteenth Century* (July), **16**

Hardy, A., Harvie, R. and Koestler, A. (1973). *The Challenge of Chance*. (London: Hutchinson)

6

Human Communication: Values, Choice and Courage in a World of Chance

COLIN CHERRY

'INNER' AND 'OUTER' WORLDS; THE SUBJECT–OBJECT CLEAVAGE

Among the changes in attitude and thinking that developed during the Renaissance, say at the time of Erasmus (1466–1536), was an enhanced separation of the so-called 'inner' and 'outer' worlds (see Huizinga, 1957), leading to strengthened dominance of the ethic of objectivity, which governs so much of our thinking in the industrial countries today. Man became no longer *of* the world; he was henceforth *in* the world.

Objectivity requires us to distinguish two interpretations of the word *feeling* – 'feeling as *sensation*' (hot, cold, rough, smooth, etc.) and 'feeling as *emotion*' (anger, irritation, pleasure, etc.). Similarly, when speaking of our other sensory experiences, of sight, hearing, etc., linguistically we distinguish between sensory and emotional aspects of those experiences, although experientially they cannot be separated. Most generally, any object of our attentions inherently embodies our valuation of it.

The philosopher Collingwood (1938) has observed that 'feeling as *sensation*' and 'feeling as *emotion*' are really one unified experience. Thus a 'beautiful blue' is one not two distinct experiences – as indeed is a 'nasty smell'. Referring to the evidence of colour symbolism of the Middle Ages (Huizinga, 1924), Collingwood argued that, at that period of history, people would not have been conscious of seeing a colour (sensation) and feeling a certain emotion as being separate. He argued too that neither do children today, nor artists. The habit of referring to sensation and emotion as separate experiences is particularly strong today amongst educated people of European culture.

During the Renaissance, the growth of physical science came to flourish upon its ground of objectivity, fertilized by experimentation upon the 'outside' world. Such was its phenomenal success within its relevant, though specific, sphere that it became a symbol of correct thinking and attitude. During the industrial expansion of the nineteenth and twentieth centuries, the economic drive led to objectivity becoming the dominant ethic in education; to be rational required one to be 'objective', as a duty, as part of the work-ethic. The examination motive compelled intellectual development at the price of emotional development, as though the two can be separated; for emotion must always precede reason – one's ability to reason (in various senses of that word) depends upon one's emotional state, one's feelings, attitudes and moods.

Of course, the idea that the world is 'out there' is a conceptual convenience, which serves our practical purposes. We are nevertheless aware that there is always a nexus between ourselves and the objects of our attention, as the Existentialists have stressed. We cannot regard the world as 'out there' in our daily attitudes and experience, for we cannot be unconcerned, unrelated, irresponsible – we are 'involved'. The 'inner' and 'outer' world separation is not a categorical distinction, for they are united in experience. The distinction is merely a convenient way of speaking; a convenient premise upon which to build so much of our thinking in the 'modern' world.

This goal of objectivity has been pursued so successfully that our understanding of the so-called 'outside' or 'physical' world has vastly outstripped our understanding of other areas of human concern; in particular, all those spheres which inherently involve human values – politics, human rights, crime and punishment – even, though to a lesser extent, certain aspects of economics and psychology.

It is argued here that many problems concerning human communication too cannot be understood objectively. Studies in these and other spheres of urgent concern are sometimes laughingly referred to as the 'inexact sciences'. They evolved later than the physical sciences for their investigation is (in a sense) more difficult. They inherently involve consideration of human values, especially moral values, and hence cannot be simplified by the convenient separation of the 'inner' and 'outer' worlds. Within these spheres of social concern, Man cannot always be considered, meaningfully, as an object *in* the world, but only as a person *of* his world; *of* his environment, *of* his culture and upbringing, *of* his society and its history.

Separation of the 'inner' and 'outer' worlds, so fruitful within the intellectual sphere, is not an assumption that we carry over often and consciously into our daily affairs. We do not carry this distinction when we display *responsibility*, or *morality*, or *cultural values*, or when we wonder about the source of *authority* or *power*, for all such involve people's beliefs and feelings; nor indeed in most of our routine, non-critical thinking and behaviour.

My own standpoint, expressed unambiguously, is that subjective matters are not to be dismissed as unworthy of consideration – even within scientific method – and that there is always a nexus between the 'inner' and 'outer' worlds, between ourselves and the objects of our attention, which must not be broken if we are to understand many urgent concerns about human behaviour. The subject–object cleavage may have been most prominent during the late nineteenth century, when confidence in physical science as an interpreter of the world was probably at its height. However, in more recent times, we have been humbled, and two World Wars have drawn increased scientific attention to problems of human values. 'Subjectivity' is no longer scientifically indecent; but it needs to be reckoned with carefully.

John Cohen, whilst at the University of Manchester, has devoted a great part of his life to rational studies of subjective matters, especially to the ideas of *subjective probability* and their relevance to various psychological problems. In this chapter, I wish merely to remark upon the value of such ideas to our understanding of human communication – the basis of both our social relationships and our self-awareness.

There may be some individuals who will still talk of 'man as only a machine' – or, to be more charitable, who speak of human behaviour as though they believed this. But I doubt whether they act throughout each day as though they do. If they insist on saying that they do believe that 'man is only a machine' then, of course, they could be challenged as believing in slavery, for that is precisely what a slave is. The test of whether an hypothesis such as 'man is only a machine' is really held as a belief by a man would best be a moral test, rather than a physical one. For the next step would be to propose the hypothesis that 'woman is also only a machine' – an hypothesis that could be experimentally tested by asking the question: 'Have you told your wife?'

A purely mechanistic view seems inadequate for understanding many problems of human communication. For example, Information Theory, evolved within the objective tradition, is expressed in terms of physical observables. In my opinion, it has contributed very little, if anything, to our understanding of how human beings communicate (though it has been of considerable value for the design and assessment of technical apparatus – e.g. telephone/telegraph systems where its main outcomes have been in the improvement of coding techniques).

Information Theory as expressed in terms of physical elements (signs) and their relative frequencies (objective probabilities) ignores meaning (symbolic values). For example, consider the words printed on this page; they could be described in terms of physical variables such as the chemical constituents of the ink, the geometric shapes of the letters, etc., etc. The physical science approach is expressed in terms of such variables but totally ignores the *symbolic values* of the observed elements. This cannot be said to be right or wrong. It is merely a restriction upon the assumptions on which physical knowledge is based, and a restriction which necessarily constrains its spheres of relevance – as, indeed, all systems of thought must be constrained within some bounds or other.

There may be some who would argue that, given time and patience, one day we may explain people's responses to signs and symbols (i.e. meaning) in terms of the structures of our nervous systems, that is 'objectively', but at present we are not within light-years of doing this. It is an easy thing to say that ultimately 'subjective' phenomena will be explained 'objectively', and this may well be an ideal for some people but, if this ever is achieved, it will not have been a triumph for objectivity, for it will presumably have been reached through consideration of subjective results. Rather, it will mean that the nexus has been closed – that the objective and the subjective have merged. In the meantime, there are whole spheres of importance that require us to take the so-called subjective view.

PHYSICAL CAUSATION AND SYMBOLIC CAUSATION

Taking the view that, at present, the nexus has not been closed, requires us to distinguish two kinds of causation – physical causation and symbolic causation. Most simply, there are two distinct ways by which I can get you lying on the floor. I can knock you down, whereby you will describe a neat trajectory according to Newton's Laws of Motion until you are flat on your back, or I can ask you to lie down. In both cases, you reach a prone position. But what happens next is the important thing. For in the first case you will leap to your feet and punch me on the nose (which is not predicted by Newton's Laws of Motion) and, in the second case, you may sit up and ask me what I am up to.

Put another way, in the first case you had no *choice* about lying on the floor and in the second case you did – you could reflect, question, argue, agree, refuse, decide, or do many other things. To debate such phenomena we must go beyond Newton's Laws of Motion, which apply only to inanimate objects and, in so doing, we shall be required to reckon with such concepts as 'intelligence' or 'meaning'.

The use of the word *law* (as in Newton's 'Laws') is interesting. 'Laws of Nature'? Who or what obeys them? Clearly inanimate objects cannot be said to 'obey'. It is not the physical objects themselves that obey Nature's Laws, but rather it is we ourselves who do when we speak about those objects. The laws are indeed 'statutes', obeyed by the community of scientists. Those who break them are punished by being cast out (or occasionally accepted as reformers if they are intellectually able and brave enough to challenge the accepted laws).

Let us return to the two forms of causation – physical and symbolic causation – but with a less violent example. Suppose you are sitting quietly, when a sound falls upon your ears. Such a stimulus, when perceived, is perceived *as* something. It cannot be regarded neutrally, without significance, however trivial. Once accepted as significant, it becomes a *sign*. Next, a second and vital decision is made in your brain: was that sound uttered by another human being or not? For if it is accepted as somebody speaking, you will seek to interpret its *meaning*. If it was heard as a creaking door or rattling window, something of non-human origin, you will seek its *cause*, but you will not seek its meaning, nor reply to it, nor attribute intentions to the door or window. Again, the former decision sets you into human relation to another person, demanding not only interpretation or meaning, but involving also your morality and values. It is an I–thou, not an I–it, relation. Such a primary decision 'person or not?' underlies all that follows. Anyone who has ever walked into a lamp-post and apologized knows why he feels such a fool.

COMMUNICATION AS 'SHARING'

It was Charles Sanders Peirce (1839–1914) who first clearly laid the foundation of the Theory of Signs (semiotics) by starting with the concept of a *sign* – a stimulus that is regarded as significant (Gallie, 1952). What gives a mere stimulus the status of signhood? The answer is that the person does who attributes meaning to it. The stimulus may either be uttered by a person intending it as a sign or not; or the stimulus may be accepted by another person as a sign or not. People are inherently involved. Peirce went on to enquire into how signs work. He enquired into 'meaning'. Because the persons are inherently involved, the subjective–objective gap must be bridged, and Peirce's concept of a *sign* did this neatly. It did it, not by enquiring into the person's thoughts or feelings or subjective imagery directly, but by regarding a sign as 'evidence of another mind'. He argued that any sign requires another (response) sign 'to interpret it'. Most simply, if I say something to you, the meaningfulness of that remark (sign) to you is revealed to the observer by your reply (a second, interpretive sign). Again that reply of yours acts similarly upon me as a further sign. It is no use you merely repeating what I say, for such a 'reply' would give no indication of your mental state (meaning, to you); a tape recorder could do that equally well. Your reply must be different, and interpret mine.

Peirce was opposed to Descartes (1596–1650), especially to the latter's idea of *connoissances directes*[1]: 'intuitions' (Descartes, 1641). Knowledge, Peirce argued, derives from the process of inference. All perceptions, all that we know, are hypotheses which are to be tested. In that sense, the meanings attributed to remarks are hypotheses which are tested by the replies. Our knowledge, Peirce argued, comes from inference, starting with hypotheses or premises which themselves are the consequence of previous inference . . . and so back and back . . . to childhood. When does the process start? Peirce argued – never! It proceeds back through your mother who first taught you words and language and all your initial sign-usage (by which you know your own thoughts) and so on back through your ancestry.

Knowledge thus is a social thing, including knowledge of yourself – which is fundamentally no different in nature from your knowledge of other people. *Human communication is a process of sharing* (from the Latin *communico*), not a process of 'sending messages' (Cherry, 1957). We may read similar thoughts in the mind of Durkheim (1964), who argued that a person is the creation of his society. We see it in Benjamin Lee Whorf, as the idea that our language conditions our particular perceptions of the world (Carrol, 1964). We see it in Martin Heidegger, in his view that human life is a 'being-with-others' (Heidegger, 1927). Man has conscious existence and knowledge only by virtue of his sign-usage, especially that of language, and that sign-usage is shared socially.

THE BAYESIAN MODEL OF INFERENCE AND INFORMATION THEORY

Information Theory is a mathematical theory that does not purport to consider meaning. Thus, in the light of all that has just been said, it is not strictly a theory of *communication*. It is based upon a Bayesian model of inference in terms of the relative frequencies of the members of a finite set or ensemble. If the theory is applied to communication channels, the members of the set or ensemble may well be signs (e.g. letters of the alphabet) but no aspects of their signhood are of any interest in the theory. The theory is not concerned with 'meaning'.

The Bayesian argument[2] goes: If in some noisy communication channel a signal S is received, at some particular moment, all that the receiver can do is to estimate the relative likelihoods of the 'message' being one out of a set (a, b, c, d, e, . . . n) of possible messages. The signal S merely constitutes *evidence*. Let $P(S,x)$ denote the probability of that received noisy signal S being the result of any particular message x out of the set. Then:

$$P(S,x) = P(S) \,.\, P_S(x) = P(x) \,.\, P_x(S)$$

Where the probabilities are relative frequencies, assumed to be known, then:

$$P_S(x) = \frac{P(x)}{P(S)} \cdot P_x(S)$$

But $P(S)$ has a numerical value, say $1/K$, and $P_x(S)$ is strictly not a probability distribution because S is fixed and it is the suffix that varies. That is $P_x(S)$ is a likelihood, $L(x)$, function of x.

We may then write:

$$P_S(x) = K \cdot P(x) \cdot L(x)$$

which, being interpreted, says: 'Given a received signal S, the probability that any message x of the given set was sent is proportional to (i) its prior probability $P(x)$ and (ii) the likelihood $L(x)$ that, if a message x *had* been sent, that specific S would be received'.

But which x is to be assumed as being the correct one requires a decision to be made – which may possibly be wrong.

Such a viewpoint regards the received noisy signal S as *evidence*, from which the relative likelihoods of each possible message x being the *cause* may be inferred. That is, the receipt of a signal converts a prior probability distribution $P(x)$ into a posterior probability distribution $P_s(X)$. These probabilities are 'objective' – they are relative frequencies.

Such probabilities and likelihoods, as relative frequencies, are assumed to be known from past observations of this source of information. The point to be made here is that $P_s(X)$ is a whole distribution, of the relative chances of any x out of the set or ensemble being the truth. But which one of the set or ensemble of messages *was* it? Was it a, or b, or c, or d, or e, or . . . n? The actual, particular message decided upon as being the truth is a matter of *decision* – of *choosing*. And this chosen one may not necessarily be the most likely one, for its choice depends upon the relative 'costs' (penalties) of making errors of choice. Again, if these 'costs' can be measured numerically (as they sometimes can), they may be built into the process, which becomes a logical, 'mechanical' process of decision, based upon minimizing average 'costs'. But it is the human user who builds in these 'costs' and accepts the consequences of his own particular method.

PERCEPTION AS INFERENCE AND THE TESTING OF HYPOTHESES

In the case of human sign-usage, the process of inference appears to the *person* communicating to be quite different from that described above. That person does not know probabilities as relative frequencies expressed numerically, but rather he knows them subjectively as various forms of judgments. That person is not aware of performing Bayesian calculations in his head, nor of deciding 'the truth' after estimating the likelihoods of all other possibilities. When we perceive something, we perceive it *as* something – as *that* something and nothing else. We may change our mind, of course, but the perception is unique. We are not simultaneously aware of a whole range of alternative possibilities, at that moment. Intellect, or reason, *may* take over afterwards – perhaps.

Similarly, when we are in a crowded room, we seem able to listen to one person and ignore the others (what I referred to years ago as 'the cocktail party problem'). The separation of that one voice is complete. Whether we hear correctly or not, we have made a *decision*: to attend to that one voice and exclude the others.

There can be circumstances where such decisions do not immediately appear to be 'forced upon us' without question. This happens for example, in the case of suspended judgments. Then we do consciously weigh up the likelihoods of alternative hypotheses and estimate the relative 'costs' of either one being correct – as, for example, when we ask ourselves 'did he say he *would* or he *wouldn't*?' Rationality may then take over from judgment. Such deliberation is an intellectual act. But for most of the day, what we hear people say, or what we see around us and believe, are not so rationalized, but are judgments 'forced upon us' to which we give no constructed thought nor bother to apply critical judgment.

Cohen and Christensen (1970) have discussed four uses of the word 'decision'. Here I refer only to the fact of hearing what people say, or reading what is written, or perceiving an object *as* something, as we do with remarkable immediacy, before our critical understanding may take over to enquire into the consequences of what is perceived. When we hear somebody say something, we decide what he said with a certain confidence (and reply accordingly – giving interpretation). We normally do not consider alternative possibilities and assign probabilities to them. Such confidence (degree of belief) is a 'non-distributional probability'. There is no ensemble; only that one object of our attention.

Peirce took a similar view of 'subjective' probability but, as a pragmatist he regarded it rather as a 'preparation for action'. When we perceive something *as* that thing, we act towards it as such, with a certain confidence. It is when we *act* that we know we *believe* it, otherwise "we merely entertain a supposition" (Gallie, 1952).

In the Bayesian model of inference, as used in Information Theory, members of the message set (a, b, c, d, e, . . . n) are prescribed and known *a priori*. Some psychological experiments have been devised in which a finite set of alternative stimuli are similarly prescribed *a priori*, in which case Information Theory has a certain relevance – for instance, the early choice-reaction-time experiment by Hick (1950) in particular. Nevertheless, as Hick has said, even though the subject is trained to concentrate on a finite set of *n* alternative signals he "cannot withdraw entirely from awareness of all the other extraneous information continually arising at the sense organs". Our normal visual and aural perceptions, although inferential in nature, are not neatly and objectively describable on a simple Bayesian model. Information Theory cannot describe the process. It contributes little if anything to our understanding of human communication.

HUMAN CONVERSATION FROM THE VIEWPOINT OF PRAGMATISM

To the best of my failing memory, it was G. K. Chesterton who said: "Man will not perish for want of wonders; only through want of wonder". And human communication is a matter of such wonder that we feel no shame in applying that word to it. It is not the mental process of inference itself, nor our ability to test hypotheses that is the source of wonder; to me, it is our phenomenal powers of creating the hypotheses – in apparently endless abundance. We may converse with strangers, for example, having unfamiliar vocabularies and accents, of unknown background and interests, in an unlimited range of environments, yet achieve some understanding. How can this be?

A pragmatist's answer might be something like this: Person *A* speaks and that stimulus may or may not be accepted by person *B* as a verbal sign. If it is, then this means that *B* accepts it as 'evidence of another mind'. The inferential process in *B*'s brain requires a setting up there of an hypothesis or some hypotheses. But whatever the nature of these hypotheses, they cannot be observed, by either *A*, or any other person, or by *B* himself (who is, after all, a person too) until the hypotheses have been *signified*. It is *B*'s response, his overt reply, his *action*, that signifies his interpretation of *A*'s remark, his belief, as a sign not only to *A*, or to another by-standing observer, *but also to himself*. *B*'s reply, in a sense, tests the hypotheses created in his brain. His belief about what person *A* means is revealed to himself by his readiness to act on that belief – that is to reply, to *respond*, in the particular way that he does.

Furthermore, *B*'s reply is accepted in turn by *A* as a sign and the process continues as their remarks alternate in the conversation. From this same viewpoint, thought and conversation are akin. There is no fundamental distinction between communicating with oneself, thinking (I, conversing with myself), and communicating with other people. This latter communication, however, requires some degree of *public* sign-usage, for we must adhere more regularly to the habits of our language and customary sign-usage when talking to others than in our own internal musing – for which private signs may be employed.

All conversation resocializes us. It continues the process of learning, of language, of body signs – and their significances – a process started at birth. Each conversation is a reminder of our own existence, as a social being. Central to this process of learning and change is our phenomenal power of creating new hypotheses – new to ourselves and sometimes new to others too in our rare moments of original thought. So far as I am aware, no computer has created a new hypothesis. Even if, one day, a computer came out with some new, original statement, it would be *we* who recognized it as such.

It may well be argued that no new idea is wholly new; indeed, *as* an idea it must be signified, expressed in language or other signs. Otherwise it is a mere feeling. Ideas must be such as to be expressible in the signs of one's own culture. They must be thinkable. Having any 'new idea' is a disturbing experience, for at that moment the thinker, as for example in research work, is alone. It is as though, at such rare moments, we suddenly realize that there exists a new hypothesis in our minds, expressed in signs for us to see, which must henceforth be taken into account. We cannot escape it. It must be reckoned with in all our future thinking.

The fact that we know when we have a new idea – that is, that we are 'prepared to act' – means that we recognize its novelty. We seem to have built into us, presumably innately, the power to make such recognitions, to *choose* that idea as special, rather than another and essentially to value it. The new idea may later be revealed to the public who may accept or reject it. Some ideas take root and develop, others vanish. But I know of no principle for the survival of ideas analogous to that of biological survival. 'Human nature is almost against Nature' has been said before. Man's continual, restless production of new ideas does not seem to follow any evolutionary principle. It does not necessarily serve the purpose of adapting him to the environment. His originality of thought inclines him more to try to adapt the environment to himself. His powers to change Nature seem far greater than his powers to change himself.

SELECTION, CHOICE, AND COURAGE

Selection is one thing; choice is another. A random number generator may be said to select numbers out of an ensemble. Similarly, I can select a playing card from a pack turned face downwards, but I could not validly be said to have chosen it. Choice always involves preference, some kind of value judgment. A choice is made when it is known that there will be some kind of outcome, even risk. Choice may require responsibility. We judge our fellows by the choices they make – endless choices of what they say, how they behave, what company they keep.

Information Theory, as modelled upon a Bayesian theory of inference, considers *selections* of signs from an ensemble, rather than their choice. It is true that 'costs' (rewards/penalties) may be built into the theory, in a statistical sense, which may be optimized on an average. But the theory does not touch upon the question of *choice*. One of its early results showed that 'information rate' is maximized in a binary source (using only two signs, 0 or 1) when these signs are selected in sequences independently and with equal probabilities. But Buridan's ass[3] was in a very different position, when stationed midway between two equally desirable bundles of hay. He would have needed to toss a coin (or twitch one ear?) to help him select, for he could not *choose*.

The binary alternative (0 or 1) has nothing sacred about it. The number 2 is simply the first plural number (so offering a possibility of selection). It is the 'simplest' selection, but not always the simplest *choice*, for sometimes we may wish for a third alternative. *Yes/no/don't know* or *this/that/anything else* offers moral escape, for there is no commitment implied by the third alternative.

True choice always involves *courage*, however little, for it expresses one's values to others (and to oneself). For this reason, all conversations, all forms of human communication, are acts of courage – however little. We choose a person to speak to and we expose ourselves to risk of snub or ridicule. Anything we choose to say that is worth saying requires courage. Expression of truly new ideas, or 'heresy', ideas to which we are passionately committed requires great courage. Only clichés and platitudes require none – for they are not authentic communication at all, they are a moral escape, a refusal to accept the responsibility of trying to communicate. Again, when someone speaks to us, what we actually hear him saying will depend upon what we *hope* he will have said, or what we *fear* he might have said. To accept that we have heard him saying something unpleasant requires special courage.

Cohen has rightly pointed out that hopes, fears, and wishes reveal our underlying belief in luck. In such circumstances, *all* true, authentic communication requires courage – however little – for truly hopeless odds offer no challenge.

NOTES

1. Descartes wrote in 1648 in a letter to the Marquis of Newcastle: "I admit that they [*connoissances directes* – intuitions] are slightly obscured by being mixed up with the body; but still, the knowledge they give us is primary, *gratuite* [unstriven for, given, undemanded?] and certain; and we touch upon the mind with more confidence than we give to the evidence of our eyes".

2. For a discussion of Bayes Theorem, see the chapter by Geoffrey Cohen.

3. *Brewer's Dictionary of Phrase and Fable* (revised by I. H. Evans and published as a Centenary Edition in 1970 by Cassell, London) denies authorship of the sophism: "If a hungry ass were placed exactly between two haystacks in every respect equal, it would starve to death, because there would be no motive why it should go to one rather than to the other" to John Buridan (*d.* 1358), a follower of William of Occam's Modernist development of the philosophical tradition of Scholasticism. Cohen and Cooper (1961) have contrasted the dilemma of 'Buridan's' ass with that of "the ass of Balaam who found [herself] in what is now called an 'avoidance–avoidance' situation, unlike the 'approach–approach' situation of Buridan's ass. Balaam's ass could not advance, nor retreat ... whatever she did she encountered threats from an angel armed with a sword or blows from her master". For a full account of the incident and its resolution, see the Old Testament of the Bible, *Numbers*, Chapter 22, Verses 21–33.

BIBLIOGRAPHY

Carrol, J. B. (ed.) (1964). *Language, Thought and Reality: The Selected Writings of Benjamin Lee Whorf.* (Cambridge, Massachusetts: MIT Press) (first published 1941)

Cherry, E. C. (1957). *On Human Communication.* (Cambridge, Massachusetts: MIT Press) (revised and expanded edition, 1978)

Cohen, J. and Christensen, I. P. (1970). *Information and Choice.* (Edinburgh: Oliver and Boyd)

Cohen, J. and Cooper, P. (1961). A model for choice in equiprobable situations. *Acta Psychologica*, **18,** 181–200

Collingwood, R. G. (1938). *The Principles of Art.* (Oxford University Press) (paperback edition published 1958)

Descartes, R. Meditations (1641). In *Oeuvres de Descartes.* Published in 12 volumes by Ch. Adam and P. Tannery, Paris, 1897–1910 (see: *Discourse on Method; Meditations; Rules for the Direction of the Mind* in a translation by L. J. Lafleur published in 1950)

Durkheim, E. (1964). *The Rules of Sociological Method.* (Glencoe, Illinois: Free Press)

Gallie, W. B. (1952). *Peirce and Pragmatism.* (Harmondsworth: Pelican) (republished New York: Dover Press, 1966)

Heidegger, M. (1967). *Being and Time.* (Oxford: Blackwell) (first published 1927)

Hick, W. E. (1950). Information theory in psychology. Paper presented to the 1st London Symposium on Information Theory (and see: *Transactions of the Institute of Radio Engineers – Professional Group on Information Theory*, New York, 1953)

Huizinga, J. (1924). *The Waning of the Middle Ages.* (London: Arnold) (see especially chapter 15)

Huizinga, J. (1957). *Erasmus and the Age of Reformation.* (New York: Harper)

7

Decision-making as a Discourse

J. S. BRUNER

Decision-making is a topic that, formally defined, has achieved its own numbered section in the library, has developed its own theorists and, indeed, even its own revisionists – if Kahneman and Tversky (1973) can be so called. Cohen (1964; 1972a, 1972b) has bravely challenged the 'reality in human behaviour' of some of the concepts used in decision theory. But while, so to speak, I have many friends among the decision theorists, I have never self-consciously contributed to their enterprise, save perhaps negatively to urge that their formalisms are often based on impossible psychological assumptions, as for example, the insistence upon independent estimates of value and probability in the figuring of utility. But that is all rather amateur and peripheral.

My own decision space concerning my contribution[1] seemed dauntingly large. Which of the myriad aspects of the decision process should I discuss? Who, after all, does *not* deal with one or another aspect of decision-making? Colleagues who work in detection theory or in psychophysics surely do: is a signal present or absent, is one magnitude larger or smaller than another? Or at the other end of the psychological spectrum, there are those who study moral judgment and altruism, forever studying the conditions under which one tells a white lie or faces the music, or dives into a pool to save a friend or stranger. Nor is the range all theoretical. In Stockholm I found a psychologist friend on the Prime Minister's Commission for the Year 2000 coping with the assumptions upon which to make decisions about the development of human resources for the end of the century. All of them, in one way or another, were dealing with problems that had, in Wittgenstein's sense, a 'family resemblance' (Wittgenstein, 1953): they were trying to estimate probabilities; to establish relative values of alternative outcomes; to be conscious of the kinds of information that went into both of these forms of reckoning; to be mindful of criteria of choice; and so on. What could I add?

But as I thought more about the matter, perhaps prompted by my own preoccupation with the nature and development of language and its role in cognitive functioning, I became increasingly concerned with something I felt to be missing in most of this work. For in fact, most decision processes I had observed were highly verbal affairs, the more so if the issues involved were matters of social policy affecting more than the person making the decision. Perhaps, I thought, this was because I, like most academics, had been concerned principally with the advisory side of decision-making – and I have served on my fair share of advisory committees! But on further reflection, I dismissed that idea. For I have also been involved in drafting legislation, in serving as a so-called resource person for committees having to make decisions of some modest moment, indeed even in helping make a few social decisions myself, as in negotiating a face-saving withdrawal of military training from Harvard or helping draft a Presidential proposal for child care in America. In all of those instances, talk was incessant and purposeful and, it seemed to me, of great and even central importance.

I am quite aware that there have been others who have been led to a similar view about socially relevant decisions – that they are negotiatory. And I have the highest regard for scholars like Argyris and Schön (1974) and Bailey (1950) who have studied this negotiatory process with great perceptiveness. But I was still unsatisfied. For if there is some grain of truth in the McLuhan dictum that the medium is the message (McLuhan, 1964; McLuhan and Fiore, 1971); then it should also be the case that the linguistics of decision might cast some light on the mysteries at hand. Is a decision a message of some kind, an utterance of signalling a request for action or participation or compliance? How are decision messages constructed, by what conventions guided? Who is the speaker, who the hearer, what the code? Are there well-formed decisions? What are the felicity requirements for a conventionally acceptable decision? Indeed, what function, in a linguistic sense, does a decision of a given kind fulfil? The more I brooded over such questions, the more convinced I became that this is the topic that should concern me.

THE USES OF LANGUAGE

The study of language use and of its acquisition has been living through a revolution during the past ten or so years. A decade ago it was largely motivated by Chomsky's (1965) brilliant structural insights into the universals of syntax. The language learner was viewed principally as a miniature discovery procedure, a Language Acquisition Device (LAD) into which a native language flowed as input, the output being a knowledge of or competence in the grammatical rules of the language. The LAD was presumed to be pre-programmed innately with a sensitivity to the universal deep structure of languages in general, and its function was to discover in any particular native language the realization rules by which these deep structures were manifest. In the past decade, the pendulum has swung from this rather dry view of language and its acquisition to a much more functional one. The functional view is perhaps best summarized by the title of a book by the English linguistic philosopher, Austin, *How to Do Things with Words* (Austin, 1962). Language was conceived, in this dispensation, not simply as a set of syntactic rules for generating well-formed sentences and none that was ill-formed, but rather as a series of acts designed to achieve the communicative intentions of the speaker in a given context. So, if I address a question to a friend in my college common room in the form "Wouldn't it be nice to get a breath of fresh air?" I count on his appreciating that my intent is not to inquire into his theory of respiratory physiology, but rather that I am asking him to go for a stroll in the adjoining quadrangle. Neither a knowledge of syntax nor even of semantics, defined as word meaning, would give me much of a clue as to how to get the things done with words that I ordinarily get done, and rather effortlessly at that. In a word, then, we are constantly fulfilling extra-linguistic functions by our choice and timing of utterance and by our skill in implementing our intentions with appropriate communications in their behalf. This is not to say that, barring the puzzling incidence of so much semi-grammaticality in speech, we do not learn how to put together well-formed utterances and eschew ill-formed ones, but rather to note that our syntactical and semantic skills are deployed in the interest of getting things done.

In that deep sense, the use of language is part of a policy for achieving our intentions. As such, it is fraught with decisions about what to say to whom, when and how. Let me, to make the issue clearer, give an example adapted from some work with 3-year-olds by de Villiers and Flusberg (1975). Ask a child to tell a puppet whether what he said was all right or not. The puppet has three sheep and one horse before him. He points to the horse and says, "That's not a sheep". Your young subjects, in the main, will say the puppet did all right. But had the puppet said, pointing to one of the three sheep, "That's not a horse", the chances are the child will say the utterance was silly and unnecessary. Our young subjects seem able, very early on, to recognize a plausible context for denial and to be able to differentiate it from one that is implausible. They know something about the use of true and false positives and negatives that in a proper sense constitutes a policy. And they know lots more as well about how, where and when to say what.

It is, then, in terms of this policy aspect of language that I want to consider the nature of decision-making, and it is particularly upon the acquisition of this type of policy in the use of one's native language that I wish to concentrate. Perhaps by examining this primitive policy level we can explicate some of the more general aspects of decision-making with which all of us are concerned. For the major part of human decision-making surely involves what we *say* as much as it involves what we do.

It might be most profitable to start by considering the functions served by the use of language proper – language employing the so-called lexico-grammatical form. A developmental perspective is useful in this, for it sheds some light on what happens as that form of communication develops to fulfil many of the same functions that, before then, were fulfilled by other means. Two writers are of particular help here: one, Halliday (1973) has published two books in the last year on language functions; the other, de Laguna (1927) wrote *the* book on the subject a half century ago and its significance is only now being fully realized.

For Halliday, a function is some extra-linguistic role played by the use of language, and he proposes that there is a limited number of these. With a certain amount of over-simplification, his list can be paraphrased as follows:

Instrumental:	communicating to get needed goods and services;
Regulatory:	communicating to control the behaviour of others;
Interactional:	communicating to relate to others;
Personal:	communicating to express one's unique state or feelings;

Heuristic: communicating to get information about one's immediate surroundings;

Imaginative: communicating to create a symbolic world with another;

Informative: communicating to inform about or examine what is not known.

Plainly, the deeper one goes into the list, the more difficult it becomes to achieve the function without language proper, until finally it is impossible.

And what is 'language proper' in this view? In non-linguistic communication, there are two levels involved, meaning and sound (*cum* gesture). At a pragmatic level, the pre-linguistic child uses sound idiosyncratically to get things, to control and relate to others, to express his feelings. He cannot achieve what Halliday calls the *mathetic* functions by this means, since in only the most primitive way does he share a code with his interlocutor that makes it possible for him to be both 'observer' and 'intruder', listener and speaker on the communicative scene at the same time. What develops, as the child 'learns to mean' in the linguistic sense, is a third level that intercedes between primitive pragmatic meaning and sound. This is the lexico-grammatical level; a set of procedures whereby his sound system is reshaped into words in utterances. This is the start of the mathetic function, "using newly acquired vocabulary for the purpose of categorizing the phenomena of the environment and relating them to his own experience", in Halliday's words. Or, "it is the child's way of incorporating the functions into the linguistic system". Shared grammatical structure and a shared lexicon in this view enables the speaker to be both observer and intruder at once, to serve in several roles simultaneously and to enter dialogue with assigned and understood roles. The child, according to Halliday, "abandons the phylogenetic trail and, as it were, settles for the language he hears around him". The child starts by learning to use several aspects or functions of the system of meaning at one time, and spends the rest of his life perfecting his knowledge of how to do so; indeed, to achieve in a single utterance all of the functions required in a particular context.

In the end, then, we as adults master linguistic strategies that permit us to get what we want by controlling the behaviour of others to whom we must still relate in particular ways, expressing our stance to the world at the same time, creating an imaginative or hypothetical world with our interlocutor, and jointly elucidating areas of ignorance as we go. And when we reach adulthood, we are quite unsurprised to find that nobody mistakes a question like, "Would you be so kind as to pass the salt?" as one inquiring into the limits of the listener's compassion. That we do all this in well-formed sentences is surprising enough, but that feat is no less astonishing than our skill in putting such well-formed sentences to use in such adept ways. For the rules and maxims for appropriateness are surely no less difficult to master than the better-formed rules of grammar.

In contemporary linguistics, one distinguishes between three kinds of criteria for judging utterances: the already mentioned criteria of *well-formedness* by which syntax is judged; *truth conditions* by which semantic appropriateness is assessed; and the *felicity conditions* by which the appropriateness of 'speech acts' are evaluated. Most of what will concern us derives from the last of these, but it should be abundantly clear that the felicity of speech acts depends upon the deployment of syntactic and semantic abilities in carrying out our communicative intentions in the context of discourse. This sounds like the ancient distinction between syntax, semantics, and pragmatics in linguistics, with three separate criteria prevailing in each realm. But let me now argue that to let it go at that would be to misconstrue some profound changes that have taken place in the theory of language. It was conventionally the case that linguistic analysis (and logical analysis as well) was carried out on sentences in isolation:

> "They are flying planes."
> "Jack hit Jill and she hit him."
> "The cat is in the flat."

It was generally assumed that such sentences were designed to state something about the speaker's environment, and since one could conceive of few other uses for them, their meaning was assumed to be invariant across speakers and contexts. But if we bear in mind that *most* utterances *cannot* be discussed without taking into account the *use* to which they are being put – the function they are fulfilling – then the isolated sentence is something of a nonsense. As Strawson (1956) argued more than two decades ago, even the simplest aspects of utterances, their referring property, is not a property of the *expression* but of the *use to which the expression is put by the speaker*. In Strawson's words: "to give the meaning of a sentence is to give *general directions* for its use in making true or false assertions". Or to take Austin's celebrated example of the sentence, "France is a hexagonal", one can only say that the statement is a 'rough' one, not that it is true or false in itself, but rather specify when and how it can be used in what kinds of discourse to be a useful assertion. So reference as well as meaning, the key concepts of semantics, become dependent upon use, upon the language policy one is following.

De Laguna's book was mentioned earlier. I want to extract one point from that rich volume. She highlights the importance of decontextualization in the development of language – the accomplishment that makes it possible for language to be spoken and understood without either speaker or hearer knowing what the other is doing, what exactly his situation is, or what his history has been – the set of processes that makes language self-sufficient until it reaches a point where we can read messages in print knowing nothing about the author or the conditions under which he wrote. Finally, it is what makes it possible to consider the hypothetical or the fictional without being committed to a position. It is a dictum of child language that you cannot know what the child means in speech unless you know what he is doing. That is what language helps us to overcome, and it is by virtue of the successful completion of the course of decontextualization that we transcend the concrete and are enabled to enter the realm of the possible, be it fictional or hypothetical. It is this achievement that renders language generative beyond the sense of the grammarian, to deal with matters in language that have never existed nor, indeed, could exist. So not only is there a rich possibility of carrying out various and multiple functions by the use of language, but also rich possibilities for constructing alternative worlds through language that are relatively free of the constraints of immediate reality.

THE ACQUISITION OF LANGUAGE

I should like now to turn to some questions of language acquisition, or more precisely, how the child forms a language policy for himself. It will be seen immediately that we have reached the point where decisions are demanded of a speaker concerning talk, and it is just as well to approach the question developmentally. Bernstein (1971) has urged that one of the corollaries of social class – at least in Britain – is the development of two language codes. One is restricted to a local situation in which it is assumed that all speakers share the same set of presuppositions and norms and that communication need not go beyond that group. Bernstein contrasts this restrictive code with a more universal one that is appropriate for generating messages that can be designed for any group – his so-called elaborated code. Various writers have tried to trace the origins of these codes in the earliest language of children from different social classes. Tough (1973), for example, notes that even between 3- and 5-year-olds there is a measurable difference in the speech of working-class and professional-class children in the relative incidence of anaphoric and exophoric pronouns. An exophoric pronoun is one that cannot be interpreted from speech alone, but depends upon the listener's knowledge of the events being described. An anaphoric pronoun is one interpretable from text only. At this early period, Tough notes more exophoric pronouns relative to anaphoric in her working-class children. This is not to say that working-class children are *incapable* of forming sentences with anaphoric pronouns. In fact, they do so less often. With Labov (1970), we would note that social differences in language are not matters of competence but of performance. Take another example of language policy on the make, this time from a recent dissertation at Cambridge. Howe (1975) shows that working-class children, asked to justify their sorting of objects in a test, use the same number of propositions of naming in their speech, but fewer propositions of state or of action than do middle-class 5- to 7-year-olds. Again, her findings indicate that *both* groups are quite competent in generating all three types of propositions. She then followed up with younger children – just approaching 2 years of age – to see whether mother–infant interaction in the two social classes might give some hint about later propositional use. There is, of course, considerable overlap between classes. But in the main, middle-class mothers are more pedagogical; when their child names an object, the mother will more likely keep the conversation going until something is also said about its state or the kinds of actions it does or can perform. What the older child is very likely doing, is quite unconsciously conforming to early established expectancies about what one notes about objects in a dialogue, what one talks *about*. Tough's analysis suggests, then, that language users guide their discourse with the expectation of a restricted, context-sharing audience or of a wider one.

Howe's analyses suggest further that the audience, with mother serving as vicar and then the school and peers, focuses language (and perhaps attention) to certain priority features of the environment as worthy of comment. A policy is in the making.

But lest we become too concentrated upon the issue of social class, I should like to turn to a more general property of 'language policy'; one that characterizes conversation in general. Conversation, Grice (1967) notes, can be thought of as based upon what he calles a *Cooperative Principle*: "Make your conversational contribution such as is required, at the stage at which it occurs, by the accepted purpose or direction of the talk exchange in which you are engaged". He suggests that there are at least four classes of maxims that implement the Cooperative Principle, and in the Kantian tradition, he labels them Quantity, Quality, Relation and Manner. A *Quantity* maxim might be "Make your contribution as informative as is required (for the current purposes of exchange)", not less nor more than needed. A *Quality* maxim might be "Do not say what you believe to be false", or "Say only what you have evidence for". *Relation* encompasses the set of maxims enjoining you to be relevant. And *Manner*, of course, enjoins perspicuousness: avoid obscurity, ambiguity, be brief and orderly, and so on. They have counterparts in non-verbal cooperation: *Quantity*: if you are helping mend a car and four screws are needed, don't hand your partner six or two. *Quality*: if I need a screwdriver, don't hand me a rubber one. *Relation*: if we are mixing ingredients for a cake, do not hand me a good book. *Manner*: carry on with despatch and clarity. And, of course, there are various ways in which we can fail to conform to such maxims: violating, opting out, getting caught in a clash of maxims (like "Be as informative as is required", and "Have evidence for what you say"), flouting a maxim with a purpose, etc.

Since most utterances are in conversation, their truth and their felicity will not be so much determined by 'what is said' but rather by 'putting it that way at that point in the conversation'. What this means, in effect, is that a learner of a language has got not only to learn to mean in the simple semantic sense, but also to fit meaning skills into the web of conversation. Of the development of this gift we know precious little. But of one thing we can be sure: there will be differences that characterize different styles of cooperation, different professional deformations, different forms of negotiation. Any discussion of language acquisition that does not take these into account will surely end up with a non-social description of language.

But there are beginnings. One of the best is the analysis by Garvey (1975) of how children learn to make requests of other children. She segments the process into an initial *Preparation of Propositional Content*, in which one member finds some way of marking what the request is going to be about without yet requesting anything:

> "You see that hammer?"

This is followed by an *Adjunct* to the Request, like:

> "Well, I need it."

Which if not grasped in intent is followed by a *Request* proper,

> "Give it to me."

Followed by a *Clarification* if required, like:

> "Would you hand it to me."

Followed by an *Acknowledgement* or by a *Reiterative cycle* if required.

One can observe not only a growth in Adjunct appositeness in her 3- to 5-year-olds, but also an appreciation of the devices of indirect request in which each appreciates the context and can proceed without the confrontation of demand. It is a telling set of observations.

We need not debate whether anything is explained psychologically by invoking Cooperative Principles and conversational postulates. I rather suspect, along with Searle (1975), that they explain little. But they locate an unexplored land just as surely as uncoloured sectors in old maps did. Rather, the point I wish to make is that the analysis of language necessarily involves us in the analysis of social interaction, for language, well-formed or ill, is a system for getting others to do things, to feel in certain ways toward us, and so on down the function list. Let me regale you no further with accounts of how men develop skill in the use of a code for communicating in a way that gets things done in a social context. You should now have a sense of what I want to discuss next and finally.

DECISION CONTEXTS

I want to argue that the making of decisions must be regarded not only as an individual intrapsychic process but also as a way of communicating something in a social context. Viewed narrowly – in the same spirit as syntactical analysis viewed narrowly – decision theory tends to concentrate upon those cognitive processes that operate in the mind of a detached speaker to guide him to a well-formed performance: knowing the alternatives, knowing their estimated values and likelihoods, knowing the kinds of payoff matrices that govern choice, being able to make Bayesian transformations of empirical probabilities, etc. But I wish to argue that a social or political decision is *not* made with these rational considerations as sole or even primary objectives. Rather, it is made as a vehicle for carrying out the intentions of those empowered to make the decision, and the process of reaching a decision among those involved is more like a conversation than like the rational calculus. It usually results from the interaction of a set of speech acts.

In order to make clearer what I mean let me elaborate on what is signified by a 'speech act'. I lean here on the analysis proposed by Austin (1962), Grice (1968), Strawson (1974) and Searle (1975). There are three aspects of any utterance: (a) its *constative* or *timeless meaning*; (b) its *illocutionary force*, which includes not only the utterer's intended meaning but the conventions that govern the signalling of such intentions; and (c) the *perlocutionary force* of the utterance, or its effect given what the hearer's interpretation was of the intention. These are only labels for matters we have already discussed: what is literally said, what is intended or seen to be intended by what is said, and what in fact is produced by what has been said.

Decision processes involving social issues are shot through with attempts to resolve the differences between these three aspects of utterances: what are you literally asking for, what do you intend to get or hope for, and what will be the effect of what you are asking? Obviously, there are substantive issues that are crucial in resolving issues of this order. I am certainly not trying to argue that joint decisions are not about real matters but only about language – any more than language itself is only about language. It is about life as well. But it may well be, as I hinted at the beginning, that there is something in the medium that matters in reaching decisions as well. Perhaps the process of getting others to conform to our requests – which is what much of decision-making in groups is about – would benefit from the kind of analysis that Garvey has applied to children going about the same task in their simple way.

To illustrate my general point, let me examine some recent examples of public decision-making in Britain. To begin with, there are certain 'topics' which can almost be guaranteed to have a particular 'illocutionary uptake', a certain interpretation of intent, no matter how they are presented. Virtually any proposal for discussing the productivity of workers in British industry is almost certain to be interpreted by worker representatives as 'exploitative' in intent. To achieve the perlocutionary effect of *actually* increasing productivity, then, will require an indirect decision, something akin to an indirect speech act in which the topic of productivity is secondary to some other conventional intent – like asking for the salt by invoking the compassion of the hearer, but even more indirectly. I offer as evidence, though I do not fully understand the evidence myself, the fact that when Britain went on a three-day week in 1974, total national productivity remained nearly at the level achieved by a full-time work force! Another example is discussion on the topic of worker participation in management. The topic itself is again invariably interpreted by workers and the trades union movement as an effort at cooptation designed to reduce the militancy of British workers. Yet, again, under different circumstances the Clyde shipyards were saved from serious closure and workers did take over managing an allegedly bankrupt and redundant motorcycle factory. It does not do to invoke 'an attitude toward private management'; for the nationalized industries in Britain, like coal, steel, railways, have as bad a record of productivity and worker participation as has the private sector. Besides, the analysis of attitudes is too static, too unresponsive to the play of negotiation in public policy. Rather, I would want to follow the line of the linguistic analyst and ask what there is about topical selection that can overfix interpretation of intent of utterances; why must productivity mean getting the last pound of flesh and worker participation mean coopting worker militance? Will historical analysis help us? And why then does crisis – the possibility of national bankruptcy (as in the three-day week) or the threatened disappearance of a factory – constitute contexts that produce a different interpretation? Or is it the question of who is the initial speaker and who the hearer? What is the status of messages that are interpreted one way in one context and quite another when the context changes? These are very simple-minded questions, but perhaps we can make them a bit sharper and more penetrating.

This leads me to an issue I must discuss now. In shorthand it goes by the name of '*intersubjectivity*', and relates to the distinction between *utterance* and *presupposition*. Any given utterance in or out of dialogue is heavily dependent on presuppositions – conventions, assumptions, habits, etc. – shared by the interlocutors. There is, in particular, a set of rules, governing *deixis*, rules that specify the procedures for mapping contexts into the meaning of an utterance. There is deixis of time, of space, and of person. Thus, when I say, "It's out front", I presuppose my hearer knows in front of *what*, or that when I say *you* he knows I mean him and not myself, which is what he means when he says *you*. Presuppositions are based on a sharing and, as expected, Chafe (1970) finds that utterances between familiars on a set topic are briefer than ones between strangers, so much is carried on in the presuppositional load. Presuppositional loads, of course, tend not to get publicly unpacked without peril in the conduct of conversation and particularly in that form of negotiatory conversation involved in joint decision-making. For one thing, as Garfinkel (1963) long ago noted, too many queries of the form "What exactly do you mean by that?" are taken as a sign of hostility. So presuppositions remain unpacked, particularly when they are known to be discordant. There often results, then, the sort of self-fulfilling discourse that Newcomb (1947) has called 'autistic hostility'. The source of such autistic hostility may lie in the operation of a maxim of *Manner*, in Grice's sense, that bars from discourse excessive inquiry into the presuppositional background of what is being said in negotiation if there is suspicion of disagreement.

A recent work by the Norwegian linguist Rommetveit (1974) suggests yet another way in which decisions may be affected by the discourse structure that produces them. It relates to the preparation prior to a request for action in a decision process, the use of Halliday's *Imaginative function*, the creating of social reality in discussion. Rommetveit is concerned with discourse in the hypothetical mode marked by expressions like "Let us assume that . . ." or "Suppose . . .". It is a mode for engaging interlocutors 'in a play of possibilities' in which both of them are supposed to adopt a certain attitude of non-commitment toward 'real states of affairs'. Rommetveit notes that the very act of discussing such an uncertain set of alternatives often has the effect of converting 'fuzzy' hypothetical alternatives into seemingly firm, socially real states of affairs. Indeed, he invokes as an extreme example a well-known finding from studies by Schachter and Singer (1962) on the psychological and social effects produced on subjects by injection of adrenaline chloride. The effect of a moderate dosage on the single subject in isolation is a diffuse excitation – sometimes described by subjects as like the effect of a first cigarette in the morning. If, however, treated subjects are brought together with others who have, or feign to have, received the same treatment, their discussions often have the effect of giving the diffuse, contentless feeling a very specific social reality – a particular mood or state of feeling is seen as shared and defined socially with respect to some topic or target. They now may feel 'angry' about something reported in that morning's paper. Mood is converted to a concrete position by the act of sharing in discussion. We must not make a great deal of this rather bizarre experiment, though I think it has a telling lesson. Rather, let it remind us that in decision-making discourse comparable things can happen. A suspicion shared and given an elaboration in discussion can and often does have the effect of converting a hypothetical proposal for discussion into a real threat or a real temptation.

I mentioned earlier the contribution of de Laguna to our understanding of the growth of language, particularly her subtle analysis of how language moves toward self-sufficiency, becomes free of the constraints imposed by the situation in which it is spoken. I have always suspected that one of the high prices that man pays for this enormous gain in symbolic power is his proclivity to create social reality with words alone – almost a necessary condition for culture, for the exteriority and constraint of it as Durkheim (1953) noted, or Karl Popper's 'World Three' (Popper, 1972) – "Quite beyond the other two worlds, *things* and *chaps*, as if they weren't enough", to quote a distinguished and sceptical colleague. In any case, let us not overlook the ways in which they work in the negotiatory process of decision – with or without pharmacological assistance!

I would nominate as one vehicle for creating such socially real events the linguistic device known as *topicalization*. Let me illustrate its power in the following sentence, "The set of conditions that produce underachievement in the children of the poor must be stamped out. It can be alleviated by . . .". Having topicalized, we then crave a label. In contemporary Britain, *it* has been tagged with the assistance of an eloquent member of a Conservative Cabinet, by the phrase *cycle of deprivation*. Now *deprivation* carries a strong presuppositional freight. One critical element in a term's presuppositions is its contrasts. The contrast is *replacement*. And very soon the decision process is hooked into the language appropriate to it: compensatory education, language enrichment, and so on. All of the discussions that ensued had the effect of locking the decision process and its public debate into increasingly fixed positions – even the extreme one that argued the irreplaceability of genetic deficit!

Recently, on the BBC, I heard a learned Scots physician explain the rise of alcoholism in his country as due to urban deprivation – though its highest incidence is in the Islands and Highlands, and I suppose that could be explained as rural deprivation. Small wonder then that during the early period of secret wartime research on the atomic bomb the word *implosion* was classified top secret!

AN 'EXTENDED' MODEL OF DECISION-MAKING

Our examples have been chosen to make a general point about the decision processes as a form of discourse. Can we make something more systematic of the point? Let me go back to the brief list of linguistic functions proposed by Halliday (1975). We may recall the list thus:

Instrumental
Regulatory
Interactional
Personal
Heuristic
Imaginative
Informative

In what manner do these functions enter the negotiations of those engaged in making 'a decision'? If a decision is finally to take the form of a *Request for Action*, for example, it should first begin with what Garvey (1975) called, in her delightful observations, a *Preparation of Propositional Content* – what the request is going to be about: "See that hammer?" In decision-making, this step, fulfilling the Imaginative function, canonically precedes the formulation of alternatives. In Britain, it usually takes the form of appointing a 'fact-finding' commission of a rather formal type, these then being labelled by the name of the commission's conspicuously dispassionate chairman:

Beveridge, Haddow, Plowden, James, Bullock, Finer, Maud, Robbins. The worthy life peer or knight so named has invariably been honoured previously for devotion to *res publica*. The membership is carefully chosen to represent all evidently affected parties and if it is not, there is sure to be severe criticism. A document is produced, usually rather heavy, astonishingly well researched and well argued, implicitly but never explicitly political. Notably, however, a Commission, Royal or otherwise, is constrained by what are called its 'terms of reference'; these universally constitute the opening paragraphs of the final Report.

Commissions always have 'terms of reference'. The terms of reference are of interest for they form the opening move in the decision process and are central to its communicative value. They inevitably serve to set forth 'the trouble'. And here I wish to make a strong distinction between 'troubles', 'puzzles' and 'problems'. A trouble is an account of presenting symptoms. The Finer Committee was to investigate the needs of single-parent families; the Maud Commission was to investigate the organization of local government in the light of urban changes in Britain; etc. The language is rarely, if ever, selectively normative, save in the sense that the committee is enjoined to bring forth recommendations for dealing with a trouble. It is the task of the Commission to establish an existence theorem for the trouble, and to convert it into a manageable problem by imposing alternative hypothetical solution frames (puzzle forms) upon it with a view to discovering the fit of the alternatives. It remains for a Minister or for the Cabinet then to propose a solution in the form of legislation (if needed) to the House of Commons. The total effect of the process is, to a high degree, consciousness-raising, and so it is supposed to be. Of the Commissions mentioned earlier, I have spoken either to the chairmen or the chief administrative officers of six of them. All of them have volunteered that their Reports were never implemented as such. But it would never have occurred to any of them to deny that their reports had effect. For all of them know the enormous power of such a commission in shaping the social reality in terms of which a final decision is made.

The process continues in the Cabinet, or elsewhere in Whitehall, and eventually in the corridors of Westminster. And wherever it continues, the discourse is framed to take into account rational effectiveness, competing loyalties, the proclamation and preservation of 'face', the need for creating a manageable social reality of alternatives, and so on through the Hallidayan functions that communication serves. I do not wish to put forth the light-headed argument that the decision is governed by the conventions of communication alone. Rather, I want to counter the even more light-headed suggestion that decision processes are *not* seriously affected by these conventions. Nor indeed would any thinking man want to suggest that once we know how communicative conventions affect public decision, the royal road to rationality is at last open to it. I would only urge that perhaps it would help us understand better why we are as we are! And that is no mean achievement.

One shortcoming of those decision theories that concentrate upon the lonely, endopsychic mental life of an individual involved in decision is that they tend to make the decision process look altogether too instantaneous. Endopsychic theories are prone to imagine decisions as residing in too few psyches over too short a period of time. If one looks at decision as a discourse process, it will be clear, I think, that the task of achieving compliance to a decision from those affected by it is *also* part of it. I think this has become much clearer in recent years when what were assumed to be 'clear-cut decisions' turned out not to be decisive in the manner expected at all – as in the case of campus confrontations. A decision by the Vice-Chancellor or President to "order the students to leave the occupied building" came quite correctly to be described as part of a scenario – as having illocutionary force with unexpected perlocutionary effects.

Without an 'extended' view of decision-making, one fails not for substantive reasons but for linguistic ones. I will take as an object lesson the reform of American school curriculum in the 1950s and 1960s; a matter in which I was much involved. The supposed decision was to get new curriculum material produced and to get it 'adopted' by the schools. In fact, that turned out to be too isolated a definition altogether, and the effect was to dilute the impact of the new curriculum effort, even destroy it. For it had failed to take into account the behaviour of the teacher as an element in the decision to reform the curriculum. And I can best illustrate by turning to a linguistic analysis of teacher talk, for we are well provided with an elegant study by Feldman (Feldman and Wertsch, 1975). She compared the speech of teachers to each other and to their pupils, concentrating her analysis entirely upon the presence of markers of doubt and uncertainty – modal auxiliaries like *could*, *might*, etc. She was arguing from the premise that a hypothetical, questing attitude might be cultivated in students by such expression of doubt, much as Rommetveit (1974) described the matter in our earlier discussion. But in fact, there was far less doubt in teacher talk to pupils than to their fellow-teachers. However curiosity-provoking the curriculum materials, and however brave the decision to undertake reform in that direction, it was necessarily incomplete precisely because it failed to provide for the extension of the decision discourse to those most likely to be affected.

I would make one last point about the more extended dialogue decision model that I have been proposing. How can decision-making be seen in the perspective of social change and resistance to social change? And here I have in mind what writers like Argyris and Schön (1974) and Snyder (1971) refer to as reliable processes for producing social change. A reliable process is one that assures that the decision process at one level in the system will yield counterpart decision processes in other parts and that, moreover, there will be some kind of ratchet in the system that will assure against regressions. The fiasco of curriculum reform is what does not happen when reliable processes are in force. Reliable processes in a communicating system require the sharing of a set of common presuppositions. That is to say, if a decision is taken in one part of a system, it must be *seen* to be taken throughout the system, and the 'stance' on which it was taken must also be seen. This brings us immediately to a linguistic question with which we can end our discussion. It has to do with those forms of language use that linguists call metalinguistic. Metalinguistic communication has as its referent the language that is being used, rather than the world of things and outcomes to which the language refers – the codes and conventions which we have been discussing.

In folk societies where there is a high degree of implicit agreement about conventions and codes, or among familiars where the same kind of agreement prevails, there is little need for such metacommunication. Presuppositions *are* shared. But to the degree that pluralism prevails, as it does in high differentiated technical societies where the division of labour creates differences in convention, implicit agreement about how to ask for the salt cannot be counted on. Mead's (1935) masterful analysis of how the Iatmul, Arapesh, and Balinese make up their minds is a good case in point: they all know how to respond when a pig comes crashing into their yam patch, knowing that the basis of their decision on how to treat the pig will be known by others – whether by the affiliations shared with the pig's owner or by the seasonal taboos prevailing, etc. That is to say, they know not only what to do but how to justify it. We, in our more complex societies may know what to do, but we do not know how to talk about it to any save those who share our restricted code.

The answer to this dilemma, I suspect, is to be found in 'consciousness-raising' about metalinguistics, fuller explication of the language that is *used* – particularly how and to what ends it is being used. We joke about 'going meta' yet it seems to me that it is no joking matter. Wittgenstein made the classic remark that the task of the linguistic philosopher was to help the fly out of the bottle. The bottle, it seems to me, is the linguistic trap defined by a failure to understand the nature of decision discourse. I would hope that the nature and limits of that trap could be studied empirically as well as in the speculative mode of the philosopher. Reflectiveness – that powerful combination of the imaginative and informative functions of language – can be served well, I believe, by a practical application of linguistic analysis to the manner in which the decision process is conducted.

Let me conclude, then, by reiterating the main argument. Most social decisions are socially achieved. In the process of being made, they involve speakers and hearers constrained by conventions of social and linguistic usage that govern the various uses to which language is put – its functions. The nature of communication affects the social reality of those involved and the possibilities of resolving differences. The decision process, in a word, is a dialogue involving the interaction of speech acts, governed by cooperative principles or maxims or conventions. Once a decision is officially made, the dialogue continues in achieving compliance. The decision-makers and those affected then stand in speaker–hearer roles, constraints continuing to the end.

I cannot claim that my analysis of the nature of decisions as forms of communication will improve the quality of decisions made in the sphere of public policy. I would nonetheless urge that we examine the linguistics of decision. For it may indeed provide a technique for diagnosis. And diagnosis could help.

NOTES

1. This contribution is based upon a paper read at the Rob Roy Symposium on Decision-Making held in celebration of the Johns Hopkins Centennial,

20 February 1976.

BIBLIOGRAPHY

Argyris, C. and Schön, D. A. (1974). *Theory in Practice: Increasing Professional Effectiveness*. (San Francisco and London: Jossey-Bass)

Austin, J. L. (1962). *How to do Things with Words*. (Oxford: Clarendon Press)

Bailey, S. K. (1950). *Congress Makes a Law: The Story Behind the Employment Act of 1946*. (New York: Columbia University Press)

Bernstein, B. (1971). *Class, Codes and Control*. (London: Routledge and Kegan Paul)

Chafe, W. L. (1970). *Meaning and Structure of Language*. (University of Chicago Press)

Chomsky, N. (1965). *Aspects of the Theory of Syntax*. (Cambridge, Massachusetts: MIT Press)

Cohen, J. (1964). *Behaviour in Uncertainty*. (London: Allen and Unwin)

Cohen, J. (1972a). Fallibility in human decision-making. *Man: Research Abstracts*, **1**, 1–11

Cohen, J. (1972b). *Psychological Probability or the Art of Doubt*. (London: Allen and Unwin)

Durkheim, E. (1953). *The Division of Labour*. (Glencoe, Illinois: Free Press)

Feldman, Carol and Wertsch, J. V. (1975). Context-dependent properties of teachers' speech. Unpublished paper, University of Chicago

Garfinkel, H. (1963). Trust and stable actions. In O. J. Harvey (ed.). *Motivation and Social Interaction*. (New York: Ronald)

Garvey, Catherine (1975). Requests and responses in the speech of preschool children. *Journal of Child Language*, **2**, 41–63

Grice, H. P. (1967). Logic and conversation: The William James Lectures, Harvard University, 1967. In P. Cole and J. Morgan (eds.). *Syntax and Semantics, Volume 3: Speech Acts*. (London and New York: Academic Press)

Grice, H. P. (1968). Utterer's meaning, sentence-meaning, and word-meaning. *Foundations of Language*, **4**, 1–18

Halliday, M. A. K. (1973). *Explorations in the Functions of Language*. (London: Edward Arnold)

Howe, Christine (1975). The nature and origin of social class differences in the propositions expressed by young children. PhD thesis, University of Cambridge

Kahneman, D. and Tversky, A. (1973). On the psychology of prediction. *Psychological Review*, **80**, 237–251

Labov, W. (1970). The logic of non-standard English. In F. Williams (ed.). *Language and Poverty*. (Chicago: Markham)

de Laguna, Grace (1927). *Speech: Its Function and Development*. (New Haven, Connecticut: Yale University Press)

McLuhan, H. M. (1964). *Understanding Media: The Extensions of Man*.

(London and New York: Routledge and Kegan Paul)

McLuhan, H. M. and Fiore, Q. (1971). *The Medium is the Message*. (Harmondsworth: Penguin)

Mead, Margaret (1935). *Sex and Temperament in Three Primitive Societies*. (New York: Morrow)

Newcomb, T. M. (1947). Autistic hostility and social reality. *Human Relations*, **1**, 69–86

Popper, K. (1972). *Objective Knowledge: An Evolutionary Approach*. (Oxford University Press)

Rommetveit, R. (1974). *On Message Structure: A Framework for the Study of Language and Communication*. (London: Wiley Interscience)

Schachter S. and Singer, J. E. (1962). Cognitive, social, and physiological determinants of emotional state. *Psychological Review*, **69**, 379–399

Searle, J. (1975). Speech acts and recent linguistics. Paper read at the Conference on Developmental Psycholinguistics and Communication Disorder, New York Academy of Sciences, January 24th–25th

Snyder, B. R. (1971). *The Hidden Curriculum*. (New York: Alfred A. Knopf)

Strawson, P. F. (1956). On referring. In A. G. N. Flew (ed.). *Essays in Conceptual Analysis*. (London: Macmillan) (originally published in *Mind*, 1950)

Strawson, P. F. (1974). *Subject and Predicate in Logic and Grammar*. (London: Methuen)

Tough, Joan (1973). The language of young children. In M. Chazan (ed.). *Education in the Early Years*. (University College Swansea, University of Wales: Aberfan Disaster Fund)

de Villiers, Jill G. and Flusberg, Helen B. (1975). Some facts one simply cannot deny. *Journal of Child Language*, **2**, 279–286

Wittgenstein, L. (1953). *Philosophical Investigations*. (Oxford: Blackwell) (translated by G. E. M. Anscombe)

8

Normal and Abnormal Human Search Processes

P. R. MEUDELL

Cohen and Meudell (1968) have distinguished two types of search: physical search and mental search. The essential difference between the two is that in the former the individual is searching for a particular feature in the physical world (a face in a crowd, for example), while in the latter he is seeking some information that is not external to himself but which is in his mind (for example a particular phrase or word that would catch a nuance of meaning). This is not to say that physical searches do not involve mental searches – on the contrary, every physical search will involve a mental search. Thus, for example, if we are searching for a particular person in a crowded room we may walk and look in what we anticipate to be likely (rather than unlikely) areas to find the person – a physical search. However, for each face that we see we need to make decision as to whether this is the person we seek or not; that is, the face currently in front of us must be matched against our (internal) list of faces before we can greet the person as our friend or pass by. In other words, while physical searches are guided by expectations on the part of the seeker, these expectations, intuitions and subjective probabilities that direct the physical search cannot end it – termination of the physical search requires that an internal, mental match must be made between the currently available information and what we know wc are searching for. Thus, while the mechanical aspects of searching are apparent in a physical search (walking movements and eye movements are examples), these mechanical activities, like mental searches which cannot be directiy observed in any aspect, are directed by central cognitive plans and terminated by cognitive comparisons.

I propose in this paper to discuss some of the search phenomena that occur in two types of mental search: memory search and word finding, and a physical search – how the eye scans the visual environment for various types of information. In particular, I shall examine how these various types of search process are affected by damage to the brain.

The comparison between normal and abnormal cognitive processes (abnormal as a result of known damage to the brain) is a potentially useful one for three types of reason. Firstly, the way in which cognition breaks down after brain damage will have implications for psychological theory – the particular pattern of performance shown by the patient may thus help to decide between various competing psychological theories. In other words, psychological theories not only have to explain experimental data collected on intact humans but also have to explain the rather systematic ways in which cognition breaks down after brain damage. Psychological theories at best need to *predict* these deficits, or at least need to be able to explain them. The second reason for examining patients who have suffered an insult to the brain is that knowing the site of the lesion one can identify certain functional systems with their structural basis. The patients therefore contribute to our understanding of the brain as well as to our understanding of the mind. Lest this all sounds rather academic and callous, let me hasten to add that the third reason for a detailed examination of the brain-damaged patient is that only a systematic and detailed examination of a patient's remaining capacities and limitations may, in the long term, enable rational therapies to be devised. It must be emphasized, however, that such therapies are not yet even on the distant horizon, but if they are to come they will come out of hard empirical analysis.

As an instance of one type of cognitive process the study of search processes is no exception to these considerations.

MEMORY SEARCH

The distinction between short-term memory and long-term memory originally put forward in the 1960s has recently come under increasing criticism (Wicklegren, 1973). Nevertheless, for a variety of theoretical reasons, many theorists continue to posit some system which holds information for short periods of time in some code or another (e.g. Morton, 1970; Baddeley, 1976). How such stores are searched or scanned is therefore an important theoretical question.

Search processes in short-term memory have almost exclusively used a probe recognition paradigm (Sternberg, 1975). In this situation, the subject is presented with short, sub-span lists of items (usually two to six digits, letters or words), and is asked to remember them. He is then presented with a probe item which either was or was not in the memory set of items. The subject is to respond as quickly as possible as to whether the probe item was in the memory set or not. The time taken to arrive at the decision is measured and it is found (Sternberg, 1975) that the latency of the positive and negative responses both increase linearly, and at the same rate, with the number of items in the memory set. This is usually interpreted as representing a serial exhaustive memory search (i.e. the search of the items continues even though the item may have been found) since if the search were self-terminating (i.e. the search stops when the item is found) the negative responses should take, on average, twice as long as the positive responses. At first sight a serial exhaustive search appears to be rather odd – why should we continue searching when we have found what we are looking for? In addition to this being an odd phenomenon, recently Baddeley (1976) has questioned what is termed the 'ecological validity' of the Sternberg paradigm. Baddeley questions whether the serial exhaustive scanning model has any relevance outside the rather narrow confines of the laboratory setting, in particular that there should be . . . "a demonstration that the Sternberg paradigm tells us something of importance outside of the paradigm itself" (p. 150).

One answer both to the 'oddness' of the Sternberg paradigm and to its 'ecological validity' is, however, suggested by an examination of the memory search of aphasic patients. Aphasia is a disorder of language, and, to simplify, there are three different types of aphasia: expressive aphasia, receptive aphasia and conduction aphasia. The differences between the aphasias lie in spontaneous speech production, comprehension of speech and repetition of speech. Crudely, expressive aphasics have difficulty in the production of speech, receptive aphasics in the comprehension of speech, and conduction aphasics in the repetition of speech, although *all* aphasics have production, comprehension and repetition problems to a greater or lesser extent.

In a study of short-term memory search using the Sternberg paradigm, Swinney and Taylor (1971) have shown that aphasics, in addition to having a reduced immediate memory span (i.e. a repetition deficit) also manifested a serial self-terminating search of short-term memory. Since most aphasics have some comprehension problem, it is tempting to identify part of the comprehension problem, in these patients, with a reduced capacity short-term memory and the form of scanning in short-term memory. In other words, short-term memory is an input buffer used for the comprehension of language and in normals it is scanned exhaustively because, necessarily, a phrase or a sentence can only be understood when all its components have been analysed. Searching a memory exhaustively therefore only seems odd if one is searching for a particular item; when the function of the memory is to hold linguistic information until meaning can be extracted, an exhaustive scan is not only less odd but may even be necessary. In aphasics, the reduced capacity of the buffer and the premature termination of the search will thus cause comprehension problems. An important point to note is that such results are not merely a consequence of any kind of brain damage since Naus, Cermak and DeLuca (1977) have shown that alcoholic amnesic patients – who have no language problems – show a slower but nevertheless serial exhaustive search of short-term memory. This clearly suggests that the Sternberg paradigm may be tapping the role of memory processes in language processes rather than tapping some unknown aspect of memory *per se*.

Unfortunately, however, some caution must be exercised in interpreting Swinney and Taylor's data, since their results are based upon mixed groups of patients – what holds for one group may not for another, and so on. This is especially the case since it has recently been argued that only conduction aphasics show a short-term memory deficit (Shallice and Warrington, 1977). Further, while there is now some good evidence that short-term memory is on the input and not the output side of the speech comprehension–production system (Shallice and Butterworth, 1977), there has been no direct demonstration that disorders of short-term memory are directly related to disorders of comprehension. This demonstration is clearly critical for the view that short-term memory plays a causal role in speech processing.

WORD-FINDING

The processes of production of spontaneous speech are complex but may be split into five fairly distinct phases (Clark and Clark, 1977): (1) generation of the idea that is to be communicated; (2) establishment of a plan for how the next sentence is to be structured; (3) selection of constituents for the sentence frame; (4) generation of appropriate motor programmes for each word selected; and (5) execution of the articulatory programmes. Although any of these stages could conceivably be seen as involving search, the stage that is most naturally thought of as involving a search process is the selection of words to fill in the sentence frame, i.e., the subject knows what he wants to say, has produced a syntactic plan for the sentence, and now proceeds to search his mental lexicon for the appropriate words to enter into the sentence plan. This is not necessarily meant to imply that the five stages outlined above are sequential in operation – it is likely that the semantic system and the syntactic system interact and feed back on each other. Similarly, the syntactic system and the word selection system may operate in some parallel ways – thus errors in everyday speech (Dubois, 1974) suggest that syntactic plans are being formed and updated even as the first part of a plan is being executed.

What thus directs the search of the internal lexicon for the appropriate word are the semantic and syntactic considerations necessary to express the idea in a more or less exact way. In spontaneous speech the hesitations between words or between grammatical segments of speech have been used to infer the nature of production processes, but unfortunately the pauses in speech are likely to reflect the operation of any of the above five stages (and, in a complex way, their interactions), and do not necessarily reflect the operation solely of the word-finding system. Word-finding is not therefore easily studied in the context of spontaneous speech. One way to examine word-finding without the above complexities is by using an object-naming situation where the subject is shown a picture of an object and is asked to supply its name (Oldfield, 1966). Clearly, this situation is 'cleaner' than that of spontaneous speech since in the naming situation we can observe word-production where we know exactly what the response should be and where there are no syntactical complications; in spontaneous speech we rarely know what word was meant to be said, and, as has been argued, the latency of producing the word will depend upon factors other than lexical search. The object-naming situation introduces a new complication, however, in that the word is now produced in the context of an externally presented visual input rather than in the context of an internally generated speech plan. This is not a trivial point since it is well known (Geschwind, 1967) that aphasic patients may be able to produce a word in one context (e.g. spontaneous speech), but be quite unable to produce the same word in another context (e.g. in response to a picture).

There is an additional problem, since in spontaneous speech it seems a natural assumption that the idea or meaning of what is to be said precedes the selection of the appropriate words. Is this true of pictorial information? In other words, is the meaning of a picture of an object available before the appropriate phonology is available, or, alternatively, must the name of the picture be found before meaning can be extracted? This is a difficult problem to resolve in normal subjects since they are rarely unable to name a picture of an object they know reasonably well (although the tip of the tongue phenomenon (Brown and McNeill, 1966) shows that ideas can be available without the appropriate phonology being available). On the other hand, anomic patients (those primarily with naming problems, although anomia often occurs in the context of an aphasia), are often quite unable to name an object or its picture, yet can clearly show (by gesture or by description, for example) that they know what the object is. It is apparent then that the name of an object is unnecessary for an understanding of its meaning to take place. In this context it should be noted that there are other types of patients (Rubens and Benson, 1971) who can copy pictures of objects yet not only are they unable to name the picture, but are also unable to indicate what the object is, either by description or gesture. Thus these patients appear to have an intact visual system (since they can copy accurately), but are unable to attach meaning to what they see. Visual analysis, semantic analysis and name selection therefore seem to be independent processes, in so far as they can be selectively affected by brain damage.

These conclusions are not confined to pictorial inputs, since in reading, certain types of alexic patients (patients with reading difficulties) are unable to read out loud (i.e. they cannot *name* printed words), but they can comprehend the meaning of words. Thus Saffran and Martin (1977) have shown that their patient was able to define many words that he was unable to read out loud. Such considerations have implications for models of information processing such as Morton's logogen model (Morton, 1970). At least in the 1970 form of the model, access to meaning (what Morton terms the 'cognitive system') was assumed to be via the 'logogen system' (internal systems responsible for the production of words). The data on brain-damaged patients clearly show that, in terms of the model, access to the cognitive system can be made without involvement of the logogen system.

If, finally, we examine word-finding directly, one natural question to ask is whether all names are equally easy to find, or whether some names are more difficult than others. Oldfield (1966) has shown that picture-naming latencies are dependent upon the frequency with which the name is used in the language. It has been argued that this represents the availability of names rather than it taking longer to recognize pictures of objects which are seen less frequently since there is no frequency effect with same–different judgments about successively presented pictures. Unfortunately such same–different judgments can be made on the basis of matching on the basis of appearance, not on the basis of meaning. What is needed is a same–different task where successive 'same' pictures are different types of the same object. Such matches must be made on the basis of a deeper analysis than merely the appearance of the pictures, and the absence of a word-frequency effect in such a situation would almost certainly imply that the locus of the frequency effect is exclusively in the search of the mental lexicon. As far as I am aware, this experiment has not been done.

VISUAL SEARCH

We now turn to an examination of a physical search – searching the visual environment. As we have already indicated, this is classified as a physical search, since one can observe how the search is being directed by cognitive processes by an examination of the eye movements made when searching a visual scene. Such physical manifestations of search are absent in the case of mental searches (although, interestingly, eye movements often *accompany* many mental processes).

Since acuity varies across the retina, saccadic eye movements must be made in order to bring information from the low acuity regions of peripheral vision to the regions of maximal acuity in the fovea. Visual inputs which subtend more than 2 degrees of maximal foveal acuity must therefore be scanned by a sequence of eye movements – accordingly, eye movements become a very useful indicant of the central planning of visual search strategies. The sequence of eye movements that is made is not random, but rather reflects these central plans that the subject has devised to extract the appropriate information from the input. The locus of each successive fixation is determined by a central assessment of the probabilities that information relevant to the task at hand will be acquired. Several factors contribute to this assessment, such as the presence of novel, complex or incongruous areas, and a more general knowledge as to which areas of visual inputs, on average, yield most information. As far as this latter point is concerned, there appear to be biases in our expectations in so far as we anticipate that, all other things being equal, targets will tend to be located in the upper left quadrant of visual space (Cohen and Meudell, 1968) and accordingly, we tend to look there first (Chedru, Leblanc and Lhermitte, 1973).

One of the most important determiners of where we look, however, is the informativeness of different areas of the input. Thus Mackworth and Morandi (1967) have shown that areas of high information (as previously rated by other judges) were fixated earlier and more often than uninformative areas. In one way this is perhaps not too surprising a result, but in another it is surprising, since it must mean that peripheral visual information is processed to a sufficient level, such that whether a particular combination of features is potentially informative or not can be signalled in spite of the fact that the same information in the periphery cannot be identified. Clearly such processing of the peripheral input will update central plans for searching and these will, in turn, direct the next eye movement.

The search of visual inputs does not, of course, solely depend upon properties of the input itself. The pattern of eye movements, and therefore by implication the type of cognitive plan involved, varies across various types of task set. Thus Yarbus (1967) has shown that the pattern of eye movements is different when subjects are searching the same picture for different types of information. Cognitive plans for searching will therefore be a synthesis of input properties and task set.

The importance of peripheral vision for complex perceptual functions has been shown also by Tyler (1968). Tyler describes a patient with tunnel vision who was unable to interpret simple pictures (like a picture of the American flag) because she was only able to see one aspect of the picture at a time. Thus, on being shown the flag, she said "I see a lot of lines. Now I see some stars. When I see things like this I see a lot of parts. It's like having one part here and one part there and you put them together to see what they make". The patient was unable to identify the picture and not surprisingly her eye movements were abnormal: specifically, she tended to make her fixations around one feature – usually the feature that she first saw on being presented with the picture – and did not tend to explore or search the picture as a whole. It should be noted that difficulties in interpreting complex pictures can sometimes be seen, however, in patients who do not have tunnel vision. These patients can often list the contents of a picture but they are unable to give some indication of the story that the picture may be telling. These patients also have disordered eye movements, but whereas in the case of tunnel vision the eye movement disorder probably reflects the lack of peripheral information to direct the search, in the case of these latter patients it probably reflects, in part, an inability to *formulate* appropriate search strategies.

It should be apparent from the foregoing discussion that disorders of eye movement are a consequence of disordered perceptual-planning functions. It has sometimes been argued, however, that eye movement disturbances *cause* perceptual disorders. That this is a topsy-turvy argument is shown, for example, by an examination of data from patients with reading disorders. These patients may have a variety of eye movement disorders (Benson, 1977), but they are able to read some types of grammatical classes more easily than others (nouns are read better than verbs, for example). It seems difficult to explain this phenomenon on the basis of differential eye movements for nouns and verbs – rather it reflects a central disorder of cognition which manifests itself in an eye movement disorder.

CONCLUSION

I have discussed some aspects of the contribution that brain-damaged patients can make to three types of searching situations, in particular how these patients can help elucidate psychological processes in healthy individuals. I have not discussed, however, the two other contributions that a study of brain-damaged patients can make – namely to an understanding of brain function and to therapy – not because they are unimportant, but because they are somewhat tangential to our theme. In passing, however, I would like to mention some very suggestive experiments (Lhermitte and Signoret, 1972) which have identified in a preliminary way the various phases of memory (encoding, storage and retrieval) with different structures in the limbic system. This work also has the strong implication that pathological failure of memory can be due to a variety of reasons – there is not just one amnesia, but many.

One characteristic of the work that I have described here is that the information for which the individual is searching is specified to a greater or less extent by the experimenter. Thus questions like "Was this word presented to you recently?" or "What is the name of this object?" or "What is happening in this picture?" are asked of the subject.

There are of course a great many searches where the target of the search is defined for ourselves and is defined only in the fuzziest of ways – where the searcher *knows* roughly what he is searching for and would recognize it when he found it, but would have great difficulty in *saying* exactly what he was seeking. Such searches involve what Polanyi (1967) has termed 'tacit knowledge'. Polanyi describes, for example, the paradox of searching for solutions to problems (in particular, scientific problems) in the following way (page 22):

> . . . to search for the solution of a problem is an absurdity; for either you know what you are looking for, and then there is no problem; or you do not know what you are looking for, and then you cannot expect to find anything.

This paradox has not been resolved; and clearly searching for solutions to problems rather than searching for 'items' is a major task for psychology – and one which Cohen (1964) would approve.

BIBLIOGRAPHY

Baddeley, A. D. (1976). *The Psychology of Memory*. (London: Harper and Row)

Benson, D. F. (1977). The third alexia. *Archives of Neurology*, **34**, 327–331

Brown, R. and McNeill, D. (1966). The 'tip of the tongue' phenomenon. *Journal of Verbal Learning and Verbal Behaviour*, **5**, 325–327

Chedru, F., Leblanc, M. and Lhermitte, F. (1973). Visual searching in normal and brain damaged subjects (contribution to the study of unilateral inattention). *Cortex*, **9**, 94–111

Clark, H. H. and Clark, E. V. (1977). *Psychology and Language*. (New York: Harcourt Brace Jovanovich)

Cohen, J. (1964). *Behaviour in Uncertainty*. (London: Allen and Unwin)

Cohen, J. and Meudell, P. R. (1968). Strategies of search. *Acta Psychologica*, **28,** 322–343

Dubois, J. W. cited in Clark and Clark (1977).

Geschwind, N. (1967). Varieties of naming errors. *Cortex*, **3,** 97–112

Lhermitte, F. and Signoret, J–L. (1972). Analyse neuropsychologique et différenciation des syndromes amnésiques. *Revue Neurologique*, **126,** 161–178

Mackworth, N. H. and Morandi, A. J. (1967). The gaze selects informative details within pictures. *Perception and Psychophysics*, **2,** 547–552

Morton, J. (1970). A functional model for memory. In D. A. Norman (ed.). *Models of Human Memory*. (London: Academic Press)

Naus, M. J., Cermak, L. S. and DeLuca, D. (1977). Retrieval processes in alcoholic Korsakoff patients. *Neuropsychologia*, **15,** 737–742.

Oldfield, R. C. (1966). Things, words and the brain. *Quarterly Journal of Experimental Psychology*, **18,** 340–353

Polanyi, M. (1967). *The Tacit Dimension*. (New York: Anchor Books)

Rubens, A. B. and Benson, D. F. (1971). Associative visual agnosia. *Archives of Neurology*, **24,** 515–525

Saffran, E. M. and Martin, O. S. M. (1977). Reading without phonology: evidence from aphasia. *Quarterly Journal of Experimental Psychology*, **29,** 305–316

Shallice, T. and Butterworth, B. (1977). Short-term memory impairment and spontaneous speech. *Neuropsychologia*, **15,** 729–736

Shallice, T. and Warrington, E. K. (1977). Auditory–verbal short-term memory impairment and conduction aphasia. *Brain and Language*, **4,** 479–491

Sternberg, S. (1975). Memory scanning: new findings and current controversies. *Quarterly Journal of Experimental Psychology*, **27,** 1–32

Swinney, D. A. and Taylor, O. L. (1971). Short-term recognition search in aphasics. *Journal of Speech and Hearing Research*, **14,** 578–588

Tyler, H. R. (1968). Abnormalities of perception with defective eye movements (Balint's syndrome). *Cortex*, **4,** 154–171

Wicklegren, W. A. (1973). The long and the short of memory. *Psychological Bulletin*, **80,** 425–438

Yarbus, A. L. (1967). *Eye Movements and Vision*. (New York: Plenum Press)

9

Subjective Probability and the Law

SIR RICHARD EGGLESTON, QC

> Gentlemen, if you believe the evidence of the plaintiff in this matter, you will no doubt find for the plaintiff; if on the other hand you believe the evidence of the defendant you will no doubt find for the defendant. But if, like myself, you believe the evidence of neither, God help you all. Gentlemen of the jury, you may now consider your verdict.[1]

> It is reported of the Duke of Wellington, with what truth I know not, that upon being greeted with the inquiry "Mr. Smith, I believe?", he replied: "If you believe that, sir, you will believe anything."[2]
>
> (Albery, 1938)

These two quotations illustrate the variable nature of the word 'belief' and it is the purpose of this essay to examine the 'fact-finding' process as practised in the courts, and to see what part the notion of belief plays in the making of decisions on questions of fact.

It has often been said that it would be impossible to make decisions in litigation if tribunals required mathematical certainty before they could make an affirmative finding. Laplace (1840) said that "We should . . . be obliged to abstain from judging if it were necessary for us to await mathematical evidence," and the same point was made by Sir Leo Cussen[3] when he said "Now, I do not take it that in judicial inquiries you have to be satisfied to the point of a mathematical demonstration – as you require to be satisfied of the truth of a proposition of Euclid."

Even in the scientific world, there are many propositions that lack the kind of certainty attaching to propositions of Euclid, but in the conduct of litigation there are fundamental difficulties which prevent us from achieving even the kind of certainty that is available in the conduct of scientific research. The situation is somewhat obscured by the loose habits of lawyers in relation to the words they use when dealing with evidence. They speak of 'the facts of the case' when what they mean is 'the propositions about the facts that the court has been induced to accept', and they speak of 'finding the facts' as if there is some process of search that leads to the discovery of 'the facts' in the same way as the search of a prospector leads to the discovery of gold. In reality, when past facts are in dispute, they must be 'proved' by human testimony. No doubt there are some sorts of witnesses (archbishops, judges?) in respect of whom we may ordinarily rule out the possibility of perjury. But even if the witnesses are trying to tell the truth, they are subject to all the notorious defects of the senses which make human testimony unreliable.

In recognition of the futility of achieving absolute certainty, the law accepts standards of proof that fall short of this level. Some writers have attempted to suggest a method by which a numerical standard could be set which would ensure some degree of uniformity as between tribunals. Thus, for criminal cases, Walls (1971) suggested that as a first step we should try to establish a figure representing the degree of probability needed to achieve the criminal standard of proof 'beyond reasonable doubt':

> Assume that a number of cases could be found in which the evidence admits of a realistic and meaningful calculation of probabilities. The first step would then be to 'try' these cases in parallel – on the one hand by a statistician calculating probabilities, on the other by a court (if the case actually came to trial) or a panel of lawyers (if it did not). A comparison of the results might then enable us to decide what sort of probability figure is equivalent to proof 'beyond reasonable doubt' (see also Lindley, 1975).

Unfortunately for those who like to have measurable certainty in the conduct of human affairs, this aim cannot be achieved. Walls himself suggested one difficulty when he asked whether the standard of proof was the same for a minor traffic offence as for murder. The authorities in fact show that the standard is to be tailored to the seriousness of the offence: "The greater the crime, the stronger is the proof required for the purpose of conviction".[4] A second difficulty is the impossibility of assigning a numerical estimate to the probability of a person having acted in a particular way, where that probability must be assessed according to the common experience of mankind. How far does the flight of a suspect increase the probability of his being guilty? Presumably we should apply Bayes' theorem and construct an equation which takes account of the pre-existing probability of guilt (before we take account of his flight), the probability that he would run away if guilty, and the probability that he would run away if not guilty, remembering that innocent people sometimes flee when they feel that the arguments in favour of their guilt are so strong that they prefer flight to a fair trial. Obviously all these probabilities must be matters of estimation or evaluation, and to put a figure on them is likely to give a spurious appearance of precision where no precision exists.

'OBJECTIVE' PROBABILITIES

The next problem we have to confront is that even if we could give the tribunal of fact a figure that would represent the level of probability that should be attained before making a 'finding', individuals differ widely in their estimates of the mathematical level applicable to various fact situations. Moreover they tend to underestimate high probabilities and overestimate low ones. To illustrate this, we can refer to Cohen and Hansel's experiments with blue and yellow beads, referred to in *Information and Choice* (Cohen and Christensen, 1970). It is this factor, no doubt, which accounts for the fact that many laymen, and even some judges, are prepared to place the level of 'reasonable doubt' as low as 0.7 on a scale ranging from 0 to 1 (Simon and Mahan, 1971).

A further difficulty is that, for the reasons explained by J. M. Keynes, there are very considerable theoretical problems involved in any attempt to take account of the credibility of witnesses in constructing equations about the probability of the truth of testimony. Moreover, the readiness of a witness to lie varies according to the relevance of the subject-matter to the issues in the case. The usual assumption is that if a witness is caught out in a lie about some irrelevant matter, he will be still more ready to lie about matters which go to the heart of the case. In my experience, honest witnesses will lie about matters which affect them personally, if they believe that the subject does not have any bearing on the case in hand, but they will not do so merely to give the party by whom they are asked to give evidence an unfair advantage[5]. Generally speaking, for dishonest witnesses, the opposite conclusion is thought to be justified; namely, that the more relevant the subject-matter, the more a dishonest witness will be tempted to perjure himself. Accordingly, in assessing the probability that testimony is true, we must take account of the relevance of the testimony (or rather, the witness's perception of the relevance of the testimony) and the relative honesty of the witness. To imagine that there can be such a thing as a coefficient of credibility is therefore vain, and the difficulty of constructing probability equations involving credibility is reinforced.

Clearly, therefore, we cannot hope to solve fact-finding problems by mathematical means. Our standards of proof, and the decisions based on them, must remain largely subjective[6]. Hence the law does not attempt to guide the decision-makers any more precisely than by telling them, in a criminal case, that they must be 'satisfied beyond reasonable doubt' of the guilt of the accused and in a civil case, that they may find for the plaintiff[7] if they find that there is a 'balance of probabilities' in his favour. But just as the standard of proof varies with the seriousness of the crime, so the finder of the facts may take account of the consequences of the decision in a civil case.

> So also in civil cases, the case may be proved by a preponderance of probability, but there may be degrees of probability within that standard. The degree depends on the subject-matter. A civil court, when considering a charge of fraud, will naturally require for itself a higher degree of probability than that which it would require when asking if negligence is established.[8]

'BALANCE OF PROBABILITIES'

I do not propose to examine in detail the subjective probability required for a verdict of guilty in a criminal case[9]. It may however be thought worthy of remark that Cohen's (1960) researches have shown that criminal juries may well believe that the accused is guilty and yet acquit him. This is because they do not think that there is enough objective evidence to establish guilt, even though they believe he is guilty. This may be compared with the provision of the French Code of Penal Procedure. Article 353 of the Code requires the following instruction to be put to the jury:

> La loi ne demande pas compte aux juges des moyens par lesquels ils se sont convaincus, elle ne leur prescrit pas de règles desquelles ils doivent faire particulièrement dépendre la plénitude et la suffisance d'une preuve; elle leur prescrit de s'interroger eux-mêmes, dans le silence et le recueillement et de chercher, dans la sincérité de leur conscience, quelle impression ont faite, sur leur raison, les preuves rapportées contre l'accusé, et les moyens de sa défense. La loi ne leur fait que cette seule question, qui renferme toute la mesure de leurs devoirs: "Avez-vous une intime conviction?"[10]

Our concern will be with the ordinary civil standard of proof, expressed in the phrase 'balance of probabilities' in the English and Australian Courts, and in the expression 'preponderance of the evidence' in the United States.

Where there is no special reason to raise the standard in a civil case above the minimum level, the jury (or if there is no jury, as is often the case nowadays, the trial judge) may act on the merest balance of probability in favour of the plaintiff. Thus, where the question is whether an unknown motorist has negligently caused the death of a pedestrian found lying in the roadway, the jury may find for the plaintiff if it considers that it is more probable than not that the unknown driver was negligent[11]. Some judges, however, have sought to introduce an additional element into the situation. Not content to leave the jury merely to weigh the probabilities, to see on which side the preponderance lies, they have sought to impose a requirement of 'satisfaction', 'belief', 'persuasion' or 'conviction' before a finding can be made.

It can be acknowledged at once that in a case where the reputation of the defendant will be adversely affected by the decision, as in the case where he is charged with fraud[12], something more than a mere preponderance of probability should be required. But in a case like that of the unknown motorist, where the payment to a successful plaintiff will come out of a fund maintained by all insured motorists, no-one's reputation is at stake, and no individual will suffer crippling financial hardship. In such cases the ends of justice will be better served (and the tribunal will make fewer mistakes) if it always decides in favour of the more probable view, however slightly the balance is tilted[12]. Of course, if the jury finds the balance is exactly equal, it should find for the defendant. This position can be justified by the argument that if it were not so, plaintiffs might succeed against defendants who had no means of disproving their liability, even though the plaintiff had no means of proving it, and litigation of a speculative character might thereby be much increased. One might add that juries, even if properly directed, may sometimes tend to err on the side of the plaintiff, even though the probabilities are somewhat against him. It may well be that it is for this reason that some judges are inclined to ask for something more than a mere balance of probabilities in favour of the plaintiff.

What, then, is meant by those who ask that the jury must be 'persuaded' or 'satisfied' or that they should have an actual 'belief in the truth' of the proposition that the plaintiff is required to establish?

The cases show that the word 'satisfied' is capable of a wide range of meanings. When used in criminal cases, in the phrase 'satisfied beyond reasonable doubt' it implies a high standard, but in civil cases it may imply no more than a balance of probabilities in favour of the plaintiff. Thus in *Blyth* v. *Blyth*[13], the House of Lords had to consider a statute which required the judge, before granting a divorce, to be 'satisfied on the evidence' that the petitioner had not condoned the adultery of the respondent. It appeared that as a result of an unplanned encounter, the respondent wife had invited the petitioner husband, from whom she had been living apart, to come in for a cup of tea. After an unsuccessful attempt to interest him in an abdominal scar, she took more direct measures and managed to persuade him to have intercourse, which she relied on in the proceedings as evidence of condonation. Until 1963, a court would have been obliged to hold, in these circumstances, that there had been condonation, and the trial judge considered that he was bound so to hold. He said, however, that if he had had to decide the case on the facts, he would have held "on a rather slender balance of probabilities" that the petitioner did not intend to condone the adultery of his wife. The House of Lords, on appeal to it, said that the judge was not bound by the old law, and had to consider whether the terms of the 1963 statute had been fulfilled. By a majority of three to two, they held that the judge could be 'satisfied' on a slender balance of probabilities. Their position can be summed up in a brief quotation from the opinion of Lord Pearson: "The phrase 'is satisfied' means, in my view, simply 'makes up its mind'". The view of the minority can be expressed in the words of Lord Morton:

> My Lords, apart from authority I should have thought that no judge can be 'satisfied' in the natural meaning of the word, if he feels a reasonable doubt on the matter in question. If a judge says to himself: "I feel a doubt on this matter and, in my opinion, the doubt is a reasonable one", can he possibly go on to say that he is satisfied? I think not. If, on the other hand, the statute uses the words 'finds' or 'holds' or 'decides', it is clearly open to a judge to give a decision on the balance of probabilities.[14]

So far as 'satisfied' is concerned, the difference in meaning between the majority and the minority is so marked that reason almost compels the interpretation of the majority. Many statutes use the word "satisfied" in contexts in which it is inconceivable that the criminal standard was intended to apply, and *Blyth* v. *Blyth* involved such a statute; the minority view would have meant, in effect, that the petitioner would have had to *disprove* condonation beyond reasonable doubt. 'Persuasion' and 'belief', however, raise more subtle questions. When Sir Owen Dixon, then a judge, and later Chief Justice, of the High Court of Australia, said:

> The truth is that, when the law requires the proof of any fact, the tribunal must feel an actual persuasion of its occurrence or existence before it can be found. It cannot be found as a result of a mere mechanical comparison or probabilities independently of any belief in its reality,

he clearly did not intend to refer to the criminal standard of proof. Indeed, his whole judgment was directed to establishing the view that it was the civil standard and not the criminal that should be applied in matrimonial causes[15].

The difference between 'balance of probabilities' and 'belief in the truth' emerges also in the United States authorities. In that country the different states have adopted different formulae for instructing juries as to standards of proof in civil cases. An erroneous direction to the jury may be regarded as giving rise to 'reversible error', that is to say an error of such a kind that the party who has suffered by it is entitled to a new trial. According to McCormick (1972):

> The most acceptable meaning to be given to the expression, proof by preponderance, seems to be proof which leads the jury to find that the existence of the contested fact is more probable than its non-existence. . . . Thus the preponderance of evidence becomes the trier's belief in the preponderance of probability. Some courts have boldly accepted this view. Other courts have been shocked at the suggestion that a verdict, a truth-finding, should be based on nothing stronger than an estimate of probabilities. They require that the trier must have an 'actual belief' in or be 'convinced of' the truth of the fact by this 'preponderance of evidence'.

As McCormick points out, such a requirement presents great difficulties of interpretation.

In *Sargent* v. *Massachusetts Accident Co.*[16], Judge Lummus said:

> The weight or ponderance of the evidence is its power to convince the tribunal which has the determination of the fact, of the actual truth of the proposition to be proved. After the evidence has been weighed, that proposition is proved by a preponderance of the evidence if it is made to appear more likely or probable in the sense that actual belief in its truth, derived from the evidence, exists in the mind or minds of the tribunal notwithstanding any doubts that may still linger there.

It is clear that the judge was not merely expressing the idea of 'balance of probabilities' in another way, since he expressed his ultimate conclusion thus:

> Upon the evidence . . . a jury could find, not merely that there was a greater chance that the insured met his death by accident falling within the policy than that he met a different fate, but that death by accident within the policy was in fact indicated by the preponderance of the evidence.

In the State of Alabama, the standard adopted by the courts has been expressed in the phrase 'reasonably satisfied'[17]. It has accordingly been decided that a direction to the jury in the form: 'If you believe from the evidence' sets the standard too highly against the plaintiff, since belief requires a higher degree of certainty than 'reasonable satisfaction'. But if the plaintiff wins the case, such a direction does not amount to a 'reversible error' since the defendant cannot complain of a direction that is too favourable to him[18].

It is clear from these citations that there is at least one meaning attached to the word 'belief' that implies something more than an opinion based on a mere preponderance of probabilities. Although the English and Australian authorities are against any requirement of belief that implies such a higher degree of persuasion, one can never be certain that some final court of appeal, unencumbered by knowledge of the history or the philosophy of the subject, will not declare in favour of 'belief' again, as Sir Owen Dixon did.

Part of the confusion that surrounds the subject is, I think, due to the philosophers who have written about probability, and it is therefore worth while spending a little effort on the analysis of the various senses in which the word 'belief' is used.

'BELIEF'

Let me propose at the outset that the word in its essential meaning refers to the acceptance of a proposition as true, not merely as a working hypothesis, but as something which the person concerned regards as part of his stock of knowledge[19]. Other uses of the word are in my view derivative expressions implying something other than what I conceive to be its true meaning. When the Iron Duke's chance acquaintance said "Mr. Smith, I believe?" he was conveying the meaning "I think you are Mr. Smith, but I am not sure" as is evidenced by the question mark in Albery's text. This might be rendered as "I have a tentative conclusion that you are Mr. Smith. Please tell me if I am wrong". On the other hand, when the judge directed the jury "If you believe . . ." he was dealing with the typical lawsuit in which one side swears to one version of the facts and the other side swears to the opposite. To prefer one version to the other, however slender the grounds for doing so, can be described as 'believing' that version. When the Duke said "If you believe that, you will believe anything" he was, I suggest, using the word in its essential meaning, as I have described it above.

There is, however, one sense of the word 'belief', used by writers on probability, which is capable of application to the slenderest balance of probability. Thus de Morgan, in his chapter on probability, says: "By degree of probability we really mean, or ought to mean, degree of belief". To make matters more complicated he said also:

> . . . I now premise that I throw away objective *probability* altogether, and consider the word as meaning the state of mind with respect to an assertion, a coming event, or any other matter on which absolute knowledge does not exist. "It is more probable than improbable" means in this chapter "I believe that it will happen more than I believe that it will not happen".

Later he points out that in common usage one cannot speak of believing something when we think it is unlikely to be true – we describe such a state as 'unbelief'. This is to admit that the usage he has adopted is not consonant with the common use of the word. The same difficulty of course arises with the use of the word 'probable'. 'Possible but not probable' used in ordinary speech denotes an assessment of the probability of an event lying between 0 and 0.5. Failure to distinguish between the scientist's use of the term 'probable' and that of the ordinary man often leads to confusion, but there is no need to add to it by creating the same difficulty with the word 'belief'.

Presumably de Morgan would have been prepared to speak of belief in numerical terms. For example, if a person had tossed two coins, and asked de Morgan concerning the state of his belief as to whether at least one head had turned up, he would have said "I believe there is at least one head three times as much as I believe that there is no head". Sir James Stephen, to whose genius we owe the Indian Evidence Act of 1872 (still in use in India with hardly any amendment), disagreed with the idea of degrees of belief in this sense. In his *General View of the Criminal Law of England* (1863) he accepted the view that there could be degrees of belief, but he regarded them as degrees rather of stability than of intensity, in the sense that in one case it might take more evidence to displace the belief than in another.

Stephen (1863) defined belief in the following terms: "A man is said to believe a proposition when he thinks of it as true". He also said that the "desire to act and the desire to act successfully are ultimate facts in human nature; but we are so constituted that all actions involve belief, and the world is so arranged that all successful action involves true belief". He distinguished two extremes. On the one hand he took the case of mathematical science:

> If a man studies mathematics, he has a reason for forming an opinion as to the truth of any theory which he happens to be investigating; but unless his belief is true, he had better have none at all, and, therefore, he delays the formation of his opinion until he has examined every possible view of the subject. . . . The strongest case in the other direction is the case of an important, but instantaneous, resolution. A man loses his way on a mountain. He comes to a point where two roads meet of which one will lead him home, the other will lead him over a cliff. If he stays where he is, he will be frozen to death, and he cannot go back. . . . The man must form his opinion at once, and on the best grounds that he can find, and act upon it when so formed.

When the traveller is said to believe that he has chosen the right road, and when the mathematician is said to believe in a theorem, says Stephen, the word describes two different states of mind, and yet a third is represented by the statement "I have thought a great deal about it, and I believe that man cheated me". But wherever the word is used, there is one meaning in common – "Here end my mental oscillations. Henceforth, whether right or wrong, until further information, I mean to act upon this conclusion as a settled matter". Thus, he says, the true meaning of belief is the state of mind in which a man has determined, under all the circumstances of any particular case, to act upon the assumption of the truth of any particular proposition[20].

The difficulty about this view of Stephen's is that it adequately describes a state of mind in which a man may have no belief whatever. Let us suppose the traveller on the mountain has no reason to suppose that one road rather than the other will lead him to safety, but he has a coin in his pocket. Being under the necessity of making a decision, he tosses the coin, saying "heads to the left, tails to the right". The coin falls heads, and he proceeds accordingly. He has now fulfilled Stephen's definition, since his state of mind is that of a man who has determined to act upon the assumption that the proposition "The left hand road leads to home" is true.

Conversely, action is not a necessary concomitant of belief. We may believe statements without acting on them, as shown by the example of juries, cited above (Cohen, 1960). We must therefore, I think, reject any definition which couples the state of mind we are seeking to describe with the making of a decision to *act* in a particular way. Can we find the essential discrimen in the existence of some *reason* which induces the state of mind? I think not, since many beliefs are held without reason. We may, however, avoid this difficulty for our purposes by speaking only of 'reasonable' belief or 'belief on reasonable grounds', thus confining the decision-maker to decisions made on the evidence in the case. We are still, however, faced with the problem that, for some people at least, to have a belief implies something more than merely to think that a certain proposition is more likely to be true than false. We can perhaps illustrate the matter in this way. Suppose we place 100 balls in an urn, 49 of them black and 51 white. We shake them well, and ask someone to draw a ball from the urn. Before we have seen the ball, we would no doubt think that it was more probable than not that the ball drawn was white, but would we believe that it was? For my part, if I were compelled to make a bet on the result, I would wager on white, but if asked as to the state of my mind, I would say, "I have no belief one way or the other as to the colour of the ball, but I think white is more probable than black".

'DEGREES OF BELIEF'

Other writers on probability have spoken of degrees of belief. Thus Venn (1876) spoke of "the degree of our certainty or belief about the things we are supposed to contemplate"[21] and Keynes (1921) said that "Belief, whether rational or not, is capable of degree". But Venn, although he was prepared to accept the idea of degrees of belief, entered upon an argument which, when analysed, supports the view that it is inappropriate to speak of 'degrees of belief' in the sense in which de Morgan used the expression. After distinguishing between 'full' and 'partial' belief, Venn points out that if we have 'full' belief in a proposition, we can test whether the belief is correct. For example, if we believe that a certain mixture of hydrogen and oxygen is explosive, we can test the matter and find out whether we had a true belief or not. But a 'partial' belief cannot be tested in this way. A coin is tossed, and we are asked as to our belief, heads or tails?

Can we say that we have a belief as to 1/2 that it is a head and a belief as to 1/2 that it is a tail? There is no way of testing the correctness of these 'beliefs'. "If a head does come, I am wrong in not having expected it enough; for I only half believed in its occurrence. If it does not happen, I am equally wrong in having expected it too much, for I half believed in its occurrence, when in fact it did not occur at all" (Venn, 1876). The truth is that we really have no belief in the individual outcome. As Venn (1876) wrote: "thus partial belief does not in any strict sense apply to the individual event". If a large number of tosses is made, we may well believe that the result will be found to be distributed almost equally between heads and tails, but as to any one toss, we have no belief as to the outcome. What we have is a belief that the coin will fall heads, on the average, every other time – a belief that it is a fair bet to wager at even money – and it is on this belief that we act. Applying the argument to the case of a jury trial, in a situation like that of *Holloway* v. *McFeeters*[11] a jury might well have no belief that the particular unidentified driver was negligent, but might nevertheless consider that in such a situation at least fifty-one out of every hundred motorists would be found to have been negligent, and be prepared to find for the plaintiff accordingly. In such a case the jury might well be said to 'believe' that the probabilities favoured the plaintiff, in the sense in which I have suggested that the word should properly be used.

Of course, the final outcome of the discussion, so far as the courts are concerned, is merely to make it clear that if, as I think is the true position, they really accept the 'more likely than not' test for ordinary civil cases (in which no question of fraud, criminality or the like is involved) they should avoid the use of words like 'believe', 'satisfied' and 'convinced'.

With regard to the idea of degrees of belief, we can, I think, accept Stephen's proposition that some beliefs are more stable than others, in the sense that it will take more to displace one belief than another. This is reflected in the use of such common expressions as 'I firmly believe', with its implication that it will take more than slender evidence to cause the speaker to discard the proposition in question[22]. On the other hand, if we use the notion of degrees of belief as applying to probability levels as low as the mere 'more likely than not' we shall risk confusion in the minds of those who regard 'belief' as implying some higher standard.

If philosophers wish to speak of degrees of anything, the word 'confidence', suggested by one of Venn's examples, might be a possibility. Alternatively, perhaps Jeremy Bentham's proposal might be adopted. According to Bentham, it was in all cases proper to speak of degrees of 'persuasion'. He rejected 'opinion' as scarcely susceptible of degrees, while he thought 'belief' unsatisfactory, since:

> among religionists, applied to the topic of religion, it is employed to designate the very highest degree, and to the exclusion of every other; since it is not any inferior degree that will satisfy them. Among lawyers, on the contrary – to wit among English lawyers, it has been employed to designate any inferior degree of persuasion, to the exclusion of the highest.
>
> For giving expression to the highest, what they have declared themselves to expect, is, that a witness shall either employ the forms of naked assertion – such a thing is so and so – or introduce the word knowledge. *Belief*, in certain cases, they have admitted of, recognising it as designative of an inferior degree of persuasion; but in other cases, in the character of an expression of the degree of persuasion, nothing will satisfy them but knowledge – a degree of persuasion above belief.[23]

The reluctance of judges to accept the idea that a decision can be based on a 'more likely than not' standard seems to have a psychological basis. Where no other evidence is avilable, as in *Holloway* v. *McFeeters*, courts seem ready to accept the view that the plaintiff can succeed on this approach, although even in that case, two judges thought that the evidence was insufficient to warrant a finding for the plaintiff[11]. But in other cases judges have been unwilling to base findings merely on probabilities. Thus where a plaintiff sued a bus company for negligence, and proved only that the defendant company was the only one licensed to ply on the route in question, alleging that she was unable to identify the bus that caused the accident, the court said that although it might be more probable than not that the bus in question belonged to the defendant, some positive evidence of ownership was required. "The most that can be said of the evidence in the instant case is that perhaps the mathematical chances somewhat favour the proposition that a bus of the defendant caused the accident. This was not enough."[24] As Ball (1961) points out, what is really restraining the court in such cases is the initial improbability that the plaintiff in such a case would be quite unable to supply any details of identification, leading to the suspicion that the plaintiff really knew that the bus was not one of the defendant's. Ball points out that it is not only the mathematical probability that a bus on the road at that time would belong to the defendant, but the initial probabilities with which we approach the case that must be taken into account[25].

That these initial probabilities can by themselves, in the absence of any explanation by the defendant, form the basis of a decision for the plaintiff was established in 1863, in the case of *Byrne* v. *Boadle*[26]. In that case, a barrel of flour fell from an upstairs window and injured the plaintiff. He sued the defendant who occupied the premises and the court held that it was sufficient to launch the plaintiff's case that in the ordinary course of human experience, such accidents do not happen without negligence on the part of the occupier of the premises, or of some person for whose acts he is responsible. As the defendant had called no evidence, the plaintiff was held entitled to succeed. That case, however, said nothing as to the level of probability required, which is our present concern.

Our conclusions from the present discussion should be that in directing juries (or themselves, when there is no jury) judges should adhere to the 'more likely than not' formula, and not complicate the issue by reference to notions of 'belief'; and that philosophers would do well to eschew the idea of 'degrees of belief' and to speak rather of 'degrees of persuasion'.

NOTES

1. This direction to the jury was attributed by my uncle, Sir Frederic Eggleston (1939), to Mr Justice Maule. I have not been able to verify this. Although the cynical style suggests Maule, I do not believe he would have failed to give the jury an appropriate direction as to the burden of proof (see note 7 below).

2. Albery (1938) was suggesting that an earlier article on the case "prompts a not dissimilar reflection as to the decent limits to which credulity should be strained".

3. *R.* v. *Parker* (1912). Victorian Law Reports, 152 at page 160.

4. Holroyd, J. in *R.* v. *Sarah Hobson* (1823) 1 Lewin 1033; and see the remarks of Denning, L.J. (as he then was) quoting Best, C.J. in *Bater* v. *Bater* (1951) P. 35 at page 37.

5. I have discussed the point and referred to my earlier writings on the subject in *Evidence, Proof and Probability* (Eggleston, 1978).

6. Even if we could achieve a mathematical formula, we might expect mathematicians to disagree about the correct method of calculating the probabilities in a particular case. This is illustrated by the discussions of the notorious American case of *People* v. *Collins* by, for example, Finkelstein and Fairley (1970); Tribe (1971); Kingston (1965); Cullison (1969); and Smith and Charrow (1973).

7. This is assuming, which is usually the case, that the burden of proof is on the plaintiff. Sometimes it is on the defendant, and unless the defendant brings evidence to discharge the burden, the plaintiff will succeed. For the purpose of the present discussion I shall use the assumption that the burden of proof rests on the plaintiff.

8. See the reference to *Bater* v. *Bater* as cited in note 4 above.

9. I have discussed this in the Wilfred Fullagar Memorial Lecture for 1977 which has been published in the *Monash Law Review* (Eggleston, 1977).

10. Koch (1964) translates the last sentence as follows: "The law asks them only the single question, which encompasses the full measure of their duties: 'Are you thoroughly convinced?'" But the original French seems to me to imply an even more subjective approach.

11. *Holloway* v. *McFeeters* (1956) 94 Commonwealth Law Reports 470 (High Court of Australia), Dixon, C. J. and Kitto, J., in thinking that the evidence was insufficient to warrant a finding for the plaintiff, seemed to reject the 'more likely than not' test.

12. An article by Ball (1961) contains a valuable discussion of the 'belief in the truth' theory, but to my mind it does not give sufficient weight to the point that the civil standard may vary according to the effect which a decision may have on such matters as the reputation of the defendant (see note 8 above). It should also be noted that Ball's discussion of credibility follows Boole, the fallacy of whose approach was pointed out by Keynes (1921).

13. (1966) A.C. 643.

14. As at note 13, see page 664.

15. *Briginshaw* v. *Briginshaw* (1938) 60 C.L.R. 336 at page 361. It is interesting to note that the majority of the Lords in *Blyth* v. *Blyth* (see note 13 above) – including Lord Denning – purported to follow Sir Owen Dixon's views as expressed in *Wright* v. *Wright* (1948) 77 C.L.R. 191, which was in turn based on what he had said in *Briginshaw* v. *Briginshaw*. But Lord Denning, in particular, would not agree that a civil finding requires a belief in the truth of the proposition found, if that means something more than 'more probable than not'. "In some cases 51 per cent would be enough, but not in others" (*Bater* v. *Bater* – cited in note 4 above).

16. 307 Mass. 246, 29 N.E. 2d 825 (1940).

17. 'Satisfied' by itself sets the standard too high, since the jury may interpret this phrase in the same sense as the minority did in *Blyth* v. *Blyth* (see note 13 above). Compare *Seago* v. *New York Central R.R. Co.* (1942) 147 A.L.R. 372, in which the Missouri Supreme Court admonished trial courts against using the word 'satisfaction' or its derivatives in jury instructions in civil cases.

18. *Farmers etc. Co.* v. *Holland* 200 Ala. 371, 76 So. 287; *Climer* v. *St. Clair Co. Tel. Co.* 200 Ala. 656, 77 So. 30 (1917).

19. Of course, if the belief turns out to be mistaken, the proposition did not in fact form part of his stock of knowledge, but until the discovery of the error the subject would have so regarded it.

20. Compare Stephen (1863) with Venn (1876) who wrote: "Whatever opinion then may be held about the essential nature of belief, it will probably be admitted that a readiness to act upon the proposition believed is an inseparable accompaniment of the state of mind". Of course, a *readiness* to act and a *determination* to act are not necessarily the same thing.

21. Venn (1876) also writes: "I quite admit the psychological fact that we have degrees of belief, more or less corresponding to the frequency of the event to which they refer".

22. Strangely enough, when Venn appealed to common usage to support the suggestion that there could be gradations of belief, he cited "I feel almost sure", "I do not feel quite certain", and "I am less confident of this than that", none of which uses the expression 'belief'.

23. Bentham could not resist a picturesque expression. The following passage reads:

> If your persuasion falls short of amounting to belief, the priest, so far as depends upon himself, consigns you to everlasting punishment in a life to come; if it fails of mounting above belief, the man of law, the judge, consigns you, and in a manner more visibly efficient, to punishment in the present life.

In a later passage in Volume VI of *Collected Works*, Bentham says that the reference was to the old rules on the Chancery side, which allowed a defendant to be interrogated; as to matters more than seven years old, he was permitted to answer 'to his remembrance' or 'as he believeth'; but for more recent events, he had to answer positively. Failure to answer in the required form was punishable as a contempt of court unless the court found 'special cause to dispense with so positive an answer'. Modern lawyers draw a distinction between knowledge, on the one hand, and 'information and belief' on the other. For some limited purposes, information and belief, that is, hearsay *which the witness believes to be true*, will be admitted in evidence. The distinction relates not to the degree of the witness's persuasion, but the source of his belief – personal observation or hearsay. A cynical judge once remarked that every well-equipped attorney's office should have two clerks, an 'informing' clerk and a 'believing' clerk.

24. *Smith* v. *Rapid Transit Inc.* 58 N.E. 2d, 754, 755 (Supreme Judicial Court of Massachusetts, 1945) citing *Sargent* v. *Massachusetts Accidents Co.* (see note 16).

25. Ball (1961) discusses Poincaré's example of a player assessing the probability that his opponent is cheating at écarté if he turns up a king on the first deal – that cannot be assessed on the respective probabilities of a cheat

and an honest man dealing a king; we must take into account our initial assessment of the honesty of our opponent.

26. (1863) 2 H. & C. 722; 159 E.R. 299.

BIBLIOGRAPHY

Albery, M. J. (1938). Some further reflections on Re Chardon. *Law Quarterly Review,* **54,** 258

Ball, V. C. (1961). The moment of truth: probability theory and standards of proof. *Vanderbilt Law Review,* **14,** 807

Bentham, J. (1968). *The Collected Works* (edited by J. H. Burns). (London: Athlone Press)

Cohen, J. (1960). *Chance, Skill and Luck.* (Harmondsworth and Baltimore: Penguin)

Cohen, J. and Christensen, I. P. (1970). *Information and Choice.* (Edinburgh: Oliver and Boyd)

Cullison, A. D. (1969). Identification by probabilities and trial by arithmetic. *Houston Law Review,* **6,** 471

Eggleston, Sir Frederic (1939). Trial and error. *Proceedings of the Medico-Legal Society of Victoria,* **4,** 38

Eggleston, Sir Richard (1977). Beyond reasonable doubt. *Monash Law Review,* **4** (December), 1.

Eggleston, Sir Richard (1978). *Evidence, Proof and Probability.* (London: Weidenfeld and Nicolson)

Finkelstein, M. O. and Fairley, W. B. (1970). A Bayesian approach to identification evidence. *Harvard Law Review,* **83,** 489–517

Keynes, J. M. (1973). *A Treatise on Probability.* (London: Macmillan) (first published in 1921)

Kingston, C. R. (1965). Applications of probability theory to criminalistics. *Journal of the American Statistical Association,* **60,** 70 and 1028

Koch, G. L. (translator) (1964). *The French Code of Criminal Procedure.* (New Jersey: Prentice-Hall)

Laplace, P. S. de (1951). *A Philosophical Essay on Probabilities.* Paris, 1840 (7th edition) and translation of the 6th French edition into English by F. W. Truscott and F. L. Emory (New York: Dover Press)

Lindley, D. V. (1975). Probabilities and the law. In: *Utility, Probability and Human Decision Making.* (Dordrecht, Holland: Reidel)

McCormick, C. T. (1972). *Evidence.* (St Paul, Minnesota: West)

de Morgan, A. (1847). *Formal Logic: Or the Calculus of Inference, Necessary and Probable.* (London)

Simon, R. J. and Mahan, L. (1971). Quantifying burdens of proof. *Law and Society Review,* **5,** 319

Smith, R. L. and Charrow, R. P. (1973). Upper and lower bounds for probability of guilt based on circumstantial evidence. *Journal of the American Statistical Association,* **70,** 555

Stephen, Sir James Fitzjames (1863). *General View of the Criminal Law of England.* (London)

Tribe, L. H. (1971). Trial by mathematics: precision and ritual in the legal process. *Harvard Law Review*, **84,** 1329–1393

Venn, J. (1876). *The Logic of Chance.* (London: Macmillan, 2nd edition)

Walls, H. J. (1971). What is 'reasonable doubt'? A forensic scientist looks at the law. *Criminal Law Review*, 458–470

10
Subjective Probability in Sport

H. T. A. WHITING

To those psychologists who take a more humanistic approach – in the sense of rejecting the concept of man as a mechanism at the mercy of external stimuli or unconscious instincts – and to those interested in human performance in 'ecologically valid' situations rather than in the confines of relatively meaningless situations, it is self-evident that human action is constrained by *subjective probabilities* of one kind or another.

The limitations of a strictly mechanistic information-processing approach to human performance are well known and are implicit in Meredith's (1966) statement:

> Any day you can witness men exposed to information who make decisions manifestly not necessitated by the information and often, indeed, incompatible with it. It is information *selected* and often *transmuted* and further *augmented* from our internal source, which shapes the decision.

Moreover, in real life situations people attach more importance to information they acquire through personal experience rather than through secondary sources. Kozielecki (1975) maintains that there are good grounds for suggesting that information acquired by 'feed-back' (i.e. by an active interaction between learner and environment) is more salient and more manageable in the decision situation. It is this kind of interaction which leads to the build-up of *subjective probabilities* of events of one kind or another.

While there are situations in which the subjective probabilities of events match objective probabilities, experimental work on decision-making suggests that people are generally conservative probability estimators (Edwards, Lindman and Phillips, 1965).

> Men are incapable of extracting all of the certainty from information that Bayes' theorem indicates is in the information. To put it another way, men are conservative information processors.

It may however be necessary to question the generality of this statement – which may be conditioned by the experimental methodology on which it is based – in the light of the *performance* capabilities of, for example, highly skilled sportsmen. Such conservatism may, it is suggested, be characteristic of relatively unsophisticated performers in tasks of an artificial nature (in the sense that direct experience of that kind of task is confined to the experimental laboratory). In another context, Neisser (1976) questions recent interpretations of the phenomenon of Attention, pointing out that theories of attention seldom make distinctions between skilled and unskilled subjects, or between those who are trying to pick up information from a secondary message and those who only want to ignore it. Cohen (1957) in an overview article on subjective probability discusses some of his earlier work with children and points out:

> These experiments thus show how, with increasing age and experience, uncertain situations are structured in closer and closer accord with the objectivity of mathematical expectation.

Further support for this contention arises out of Björkman and Kozielecki's (1973) demonstration, quoted in Kozielecki (1975), that conservative shifts in the preference for particular gambles (bets) – albeit in a more conservative direction – can be brought about by the manipulation of feedforward and feedback parameters.

Even under the restrictions of a constrained laboratory experiment, both Shuford (1961) and Robinson (1964) have shown that on the 'input' side people can keep track of even slight changes of probability of occurrence of a signal during an experimental run.

In a more 'output'-orientated study involving football players from two first division (professional), a university (amateur) and a grammar school (amateur) club, Cohen and Dearnaley[1] (1962) were able to demonstrate the players' ability to match their estimated and actual performances (Figure 1; Table 1) when required to make judgments about their ability to score goals from different distances away from the goal.

Differences between the teams in this respect were apparent, and it

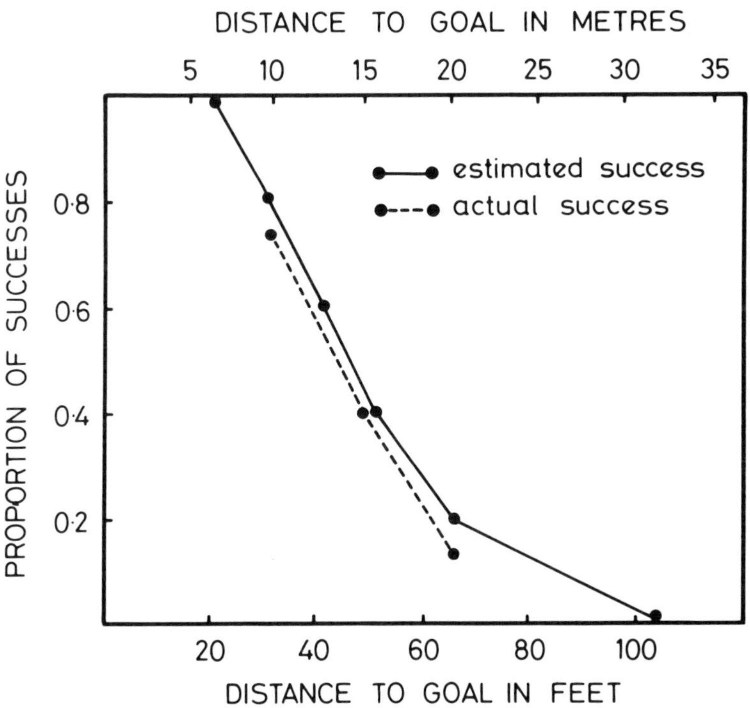

Figure 1 Estimated and actual success in scoring from various distances from the goal

might be speculated that these were due in part to differences in levels of performance of the players. At the 1/100 level for example the very unrealistic estimates on the part of two players from the grammar school team were responsible for the large variance of the team itself, which is reflected in its large mean of 116 feet (35.4 metres) shown in Table 1. Differences were also apparent between one of the first division teams and the University team. Whereas the latter players were not prepared to shoot unless they felt they had at least one chance in three of success the first division players were content with

Table 1 **Average distances to the goal, in feet (and metres), corresponding to variations in expected success in attempts to score goals of football players from two first division (professional) clubs, a university (amateur) club, and a grammar school (amateur) club**

	Expected success						
Players	*1 in 100 attempts*	*1 in 5 attempts*	*2 in 5 attempts*	*3 in 5 attempts*	*4 in 5 attempts*	*99 in 100 attempts*	*N*
Manchester United	106(32.3)	67(20.4)	50(15.2)	39(11.9)	29(8.8)	19(5.8)	12
West Bromwich Albion	96(29.3)	68(20.7)	55(16.8)	46(14.0)	36(11.0)	28(8.5)	8
University	96(29.3)	59(18.0)	45(13.7)	36(11.0)	28(8.5)	17(5.2)	5
Grammar school	116(35.4)	71(21.6)	55(16.8)	45(13.7)	33(10.1)	19(5.8)	8
MEAN	104(31.7)	67(20.4)	53(15.8)	42(12.8)	31(9.4)	21(6.4)	—

a subjective chance of eight in a hundred. An interpretation of these differences would be speculative, since the factors involved are likely to be manifold and complex.

Some of the findings quoted show agreement about the ability of at least experienced people accurately to match subjective with objective probabilities of events but at the same time to differ in the degree of risk they are prepared to take. This serves to question the utility of probabilistic models by themselves in explaining risk-taking behaviour. We shall return to this problem later.

SUBJECTIVE PROBABILITY

So far, a distinction has been drawn between subjective and objective probability by quoting examples of the way in which the two are contrasted. The following statement clarifies the interpretation put by psychologists on the term subjective probability (Cohen and Christensen, 1970):

> Subjective, like logical, probability accordingly represents a person's degree of belief in a statement on the basis of the given evidence. Such a probability is subjective in the sense that any degree of belief can be held by a person in any statement on any evidence, provided only that his other degrees of belief have appropriate values. If his other degrees of belief do not have these appropriate values, he is said to be making an erratic judgement comparable to a faulty calculation in arithmetic.

While recognizing the importance of subjective probability in determining what people actually do in decision-making situations, the inherent difficulty of obtaining information about such a parameter has meant a paucity of available information about 'real world behaviour'. The price paid for what are considered as the necessary controlled experimental conditions is questionable ecological validity (Coombs, Dawes and Tversky, 1970).

Some experimenters, appreciating the problems inherent in trying to directly measure subjective probability on the part of the observer, have either altered their focus of attention away from the topic or looked for alternative ways of obtaining solutions to the problems with which they are confronted:

> An observer can base his response only on his own assessment of the probability that the event was an . . . The experimenter is not able directly to measure this assessment by the observer. Besides, experimenters are often more interested in what information the observation gives the observer than in the final assessment.
>
> For both these reasons, conventional usage in detectability theory abandons subjective probability in favour of a more 'objective' measure which is closely related to the value of the observations as evidence.

Here, Taylor (1967) is referring to the 'likelihood ratio' of classical signal detection theory. Cohen and Christensen (1970), on the other hand, draw attention to the *restricted* utility of 'signal detection theory' pointing out its statistical rather than psychological nature. In a similar way, Broadbent (1971) writes about the 'unsolved problems in signal detection theory' which can be summarized as follows:

1. Can the evidence received by the observer be arranged on a single dimension of sensory evidence?
2. Even if such 'evidence' does form a single continuum, can it be assumed that the subject knows the value of the likelihood ratio for any particular value of evidence?
3. Even if it is the case that both a single dimension of likelihood ratio and perfect knowledge of its value by the subject are available, can it be assumed that the subject will behave rationally?

Broadbent further points out that such assumptions might well be valid in the psychological case and yet completely invalid in the case of vigilance. It depends of course on the kind of information for which the experimenter is looking as Taylor (1967) implies and as is illustrated by the Blitz and van Moorst (1977) study discussed below in the context of *Subjective Fatigue*. Cohen and Christensen (1970) draw a distinction:

> The task of the psychology of decision-making, by contrast with that of decision theory, is to study the subjective elements that enter into decision-making partly for their intrinsic interest and partly because only when their nature is understood will it be possible to improve and control them, and remove, or at least be

> on guard against, their erratic features. This approach to decision-making is inspired by a desire to extend our self-knowledge so as to understand how, so to speak, we make up our minds.

While one of these elements is *subjective probability*, it is not the only element.

In the period since Taylor (1967) made his statement, the trend towards an acceptance of the essential importance of subjectivity in human performance has not only become more acceptable, but more necessary (Coombs, Dawes and Tversky, 1970), in an attempt to come to terms with the limited explanatory possibilities in classical theoretical positions. Considerations of man – the decision-maker – as an information-processing system have become less mechanistic in outlook and more concerned with the way in which such information is *actively organized* by the perceiver not only in terms of the information *per se* but in terms of related parameters like perceived risk and utility value. The application of such models to the analysis and understanding of *sporting* performance raises many interesting possibilities, not the least of which are concerned with the time constraints imposed on information-processing in situations involving rapidly changing displays. There is a difference between the situation in which one can ask a player about his expectancies outside the game or other competitive situation and that which ensues when he is actively involved. Ricoeur (1966) makes this point succinctly:

> We must not be misled by classical analysis which distinguished the several phases of voluntary activity, deliberation, decision and execution, *in time*. Decision does not *follow* deliberation purely and simply, nor does action *follow* decision. Delayed action, separated from decision by an interval, is not normative.

Such decisions reflecting as they do on the skilful performance of a task should not be considered as the only or even the most necessary determinants of success in sporting situations. Cohen (1975) reminds us that there is more to winning and losing than skill factors alone:

> There is confidence and the will to win which may be crucial.

Such considerations emphasize the need to take cognizance of other factors of the decision-making process under risky conditions. Cohen's point is an important one in as far as such parameters, while being recognised by sports psychologists, have seldom been utilized within an experimental sport-oriented paradigm. There are however exceptions and these will be returned to later in the chapter.

INFORMATION PROCESSING IN SPORT SITUATIONS

While the importance of a consideration of information processing in a sport context has been well recognized, interpretations placed upon its function and importance are still the subject of debate. Recently, for example, Whiting (1975) questioned the *interpretation* of the 'open–closed' skill continuum proposed by Knapp (1964) whereby positioning of particular sports activities along the continuum is determined by the importance attached to the monitoring of the display in the control of the skill. The important and neglected question is 'to whom the importance is assigned – the performer himself, or some external agency?' Disenchantment with a simplistic interpretation of the continuum arises largely from a consideration of Poulton's (1950) original concept of such a continuum as being based upon the degree of *predictability* of relevant environmental information. The whole problem centres around the word 'prediction' and as Poulton (1950) states:

> . . . there can be no such thing as an 'unpractised closed skill', for a skill cannot become closed until it has been practised sufficiently often for all the relevant environmental signals to be predictable.

Predictability is a subjective construct in psychological terms. An event is essentially predictable *to someone*. While it might be supposed that the subjective prediction of events would closely match their objective statistical characteristics – at least in the more experienced human performer (as was hinted in the Cohen and Dearnaley (1962) study) – this is by no means axiomatic. Thus – if considered useful – the positioning of a skill on an open–closed continuum can only be done *relative to the person performing the skill at a particular time*. Changes and fluctuations are to be expected in so far as predictability and anticipation are ongoing processes, and also that 'stress' situations can affect information-processing and strategy in the sense that there might be a regression to earlier levels of control (Whiting, 1969) or – in terms to be used later – to another *dimension* of control.

Tyldesley (1978) for example has demonstrated differences in the dimensions of information extracted from a visual display by novice table-tennis players in comparison to that extracted by experts within the visual modality. The nature of these within-modality changes was provided by a multivariate analysis of a ball-striking task. This analysis addressed the question 'which of the various kinematic factors describing the ball-flight and subjectively evaluated by the player predominantly determine the movement characteristics of a player attempting to hit a table-tennis ball to a target?'

A relatively unpredictable ball-flight was provided in a table-tennis situation and two groups (one trained, the other untrained) were asked to return the balls into a target square on the opposite side of the table. Twenty-two kinematic features describing the ball-flight (the INPUT features) and the bat movement (the OUTPUT features) were extracted by operational analysis and formed a 'features × attempts' matrix *for each subject*. Earlier work had indicated that one of the most important output characteristics in this performance was the start time of the ballistic downswing (IP). The multiple linear regression evaluated the partial contribution to the total IP variance of each of the measured input features. It was found possible to account for more than 97% of the total IP variance in five of the six subjects when only five input features were included in the equation. Predominant among these factors were BALL DISPLACEMENT at IP; BALL VELOCITY at IP and BALL PROJECTION VELOCITY (Table 2).

IP time in *non-trained* performers appeared to be a function of both a displacement and a velocity measure with the possible inference that both distance and its rate of change were important information sources to the beginners (subjects 1, 2 and 3). In contrast, the highly trained performers (subjects 4, 5 and 6) indicated a considerably reduced steering function of velocity information with the major portion of IP variation accounted for by input *displacement* variations (Table 2). These data suggest that the expert is able to time the ballistic initiation on what is possibly a simpler information basis than the novice, who is subject to changes in both *input velocity* and *displacement*. Alternative explanations, for example that the expert *does* recognize velocity information but does not utilize it in his decision-making, are also tenable.

Table 2 **The partial contributions to the overall variance in the start-times of ballistic downswings of trained and untrained table-tennis players of three of the five kinematic factors identified in multiple regression analysis**

Subjects	*Percentage variance in IP*[a] *accounted for*			*Simple correlation with IP*[a]			*Overall percentage variance accounted for by all equation factors*
	BD[b]	*BV*[c]	*BPV*[d]	*BD*[b]	*BV*[c]	*BPV*[d]	
Untrained							
1	55	<1	39	−0.95	0.19	−0.63	97
2	22	40	13	−0.55	0.70	−0.36	83
3	62	<1	20	−0.90	−0.76	−0.44	99
Trained							
4	82	<1	13	−0.97	−0.39	−0.37	98
5	73	<1	1	−0.85	0.04	−0.12	98
6	81	<1	13	−0.95	0.07	−0.37	98

[a] Start-times of ballistic downswings (IP)
[b] Ball displacement (BD)
[c] Ball velocity (BV)
[d] Ball projection velocity (BPV)

In an earlier experiment, Sharp and Whiting (1975) also showed a progression from usage of the image–retina system to the eye–head system in obtaining information relevant to decision-making in a ball-catching task.

In any sphere of human performance, experience of the person within the task situation leads to a build-up of his *own* conceptual model of the system, which enables him in Whitfield's (1967) terms to:

> . . . appreciate the interactions of the main parameters in the system and to predict the consequences of any control action he may take.

The essential subjectivity of such models is appreciated by Whitfield when he makes the salient point that:

> . . . operators' use of these conceptual models seems to be more effective in many cases than the attempts of the design engineer to control the process, presumably because of complex interactions which cannot be predicted from theoretical formulations.

Such knowledge is obtained only by 'acquaintance'. A similar idea is implicit in Polanyi's (1958) concept of *tacit knowledge* which is not definable. This seems to have been in the minds of Cohen and Dearnaley (1962) when they wrote:

> . . . skill, in whatever form it is manifested, including skill in football, may be regarded as the exercise of connoisseurship the ingredients of which cannot all be made explicit.

The concept is returned to rather more amusingly in a recent insightful article by Williams (1977) entitled Psychobikistics:

> Consider for a moment what we really mean by riding a bicycle. There is more to cycling than simply taking a short ride on a machine down a straight road, just as there is more to language than the stereotyped utterances of a parrot. It is true that animals have been taught to perform certain unnatural acts. Dogs, cats and even elephants have been taught to use scooters and we have all seen the antics of chimpanzees with bicycles. But we all

> laugh at the animals' hopeless question 'can you ride tandem?' Of course she cannot ride tandem! There is a quiddity to cycling which is essentially human.

There is probably less dispute over whether or not people build up internal representations (conceptual models) of the systems in which they operate than over the *kind* of internal representations which they do build up. While it is true to say that major attention has in the past been focused on probabilistic representations based on feedforward, feedback or combinations of the two sources of information as already suggested, these may not be the only kinds of internal representation that are utilized by people performing in risk-taking situations. Kozielecki (1975), for example, lists three representative models (the performer's choice from amongst such models being determined by factors like competence, cognitive style, personality traits):

1. *Probabilistic representation* – in the manner already suggested, which Kozielecki proposes, while being highly adequate, is a difficult one with which to work.
2. *Heuristic representation* – in which a decision (gamble) "is approached as a multidimensional stimulus and represented as a list of dimensions" (e.g. probability of winning, amount to win, probability of losing, amount to lose, risk level, context variables etc.). Such a list may also be hierarchically arranged in terms of the weight assigned to that feature in coming to a decision. This model, it is suggested, is much easier than the probabilistic model and reduces cognitive strain.
3. *Deterministic representation* – based on discovery of the *rules* which deterministically represent the outcome of any gamble. Knowing the rules leads to decision certainty.

It is Kozielecki's view that:

> . . . there is no basis for the assumption that decision-makers approach risky tasks as probability distributions over sets of possible outcomes.

He reports evidence from a number of studies which demonstrate the use by the performer of a heuristic, rather than a probabilistic, mode.

Cohen and Christensen (1970) earlier drew attention to the heuristic nature of search strategies employed by children of different chronological ages:

> The distinctive feature of human search, by contrast with mechanical search is, in fact, the use of heuristic devices. . . The nature of human heuristic devices and intuitive short cuts is largely unknown.

In one of their experiments (Cohen and Christensen, 1970) children between the chronological ages of 9 and 15 years were required to identify two circles (known only to the experimenters) from amongst a printed page of circles varying in number between 2^2 and 2^{10} with the constraint that the only questions permitted were those capable of being answered by a 'Yes' or 'No'. Cohen and Christensen[2] identified two *major* search strategies:

1. The *element-type* (with two sub-categories) in which the child's search is circle-specific, i.e. object-bound.
2. The *set-type* (with four sub-categories) in which 'scanning' of varying degrees of efficiency is employed, i.e. particular lines, rows, groups, half-page, etc.

Table 3 illustrates the increase with age in the ratio of *set-type* to *element-type* questions from children *who did in fact attempt a set-type strategy*. (It should be noted that a possible confounding factor was the higher average ability of the 12 and 15-year-old children).

Table 3 Ratio of set-type to element-type questions asked by children in three age groups when attempting to use set-type strategy in a search task

Age-group of subjects (year)	*Number of subjects*	*Number using a set-type strategy*	*Ratio of set-type to element-type questions*
9	50	10	1.9 to 1
12	51	38	2.4 to 1
15	53	30	3.0 to 1

The ideas being presented by Kozielecki and by Cohen and Christensen were perhaps foreseen and appreciated by Broadbent (1965) when he wrote:

> . . . unfortunately, human decision-making does not conform to mathematical theory. The principle that one should go for the best possibe combination of probability and value is a mathematical one; and again one could always programme a computer to do it. In this case, however, there is no doubt that people do not behave the way that mathematics say they should do.

Kozielecki introduces the interesting term 'subjective rationality' – which he distinguishes from *substantive* and *methodological* rationality – implying that decisions for action arise out of the internal representation generated by the person. A side-issue arising from such a concept is that a person's behaviour may be rational from his own viewpoint but irrational from that of an observer. Wilberg (1975), in his overview article on an analysis and application of game and human performance theory to sport and competition, appreciates this point, but prefers an alternative interpretation:

> . . . while your opponent may appear to be playing irrationally he may in actual fact be laying a trap for you, a trap from which you may not recover. Consequently, it is usually assumed that even though irrational play may arise it is in effect a disguise for well considered and successful rational play.

Do sports participants, judges and coaches perform in a rational manner? Is it meaningful to talk about *externally* determined rationality in sport or other real-life situations? What do we really know about the intentions, feelings, personal pay-offs relative to sport participation and the way in which these affect strategies within and between competitors? Unfortunately, in empirical terms very little, but the fact that they play a crucial role in determining the outcome of sporting contests is implicit in the concept of 'gamesmanship'. We will take just two examples to illustrate the point:

> The next time your opponent is having a hot streak, simply ask him as you switch courts, "Say, George, what are you doing so

differently that's making your forehead so good today?" If he takes the bait – and 95% will – and begins to think about how he's swinging, telling you how he's really meeting the ball out in front, keeping his wrist firm and following through better, his streak invariably will end. He will lose his timing and fluidity as he tries to repeat what he has just told you he was doing so well. (Gallwey, 1974).

In tennis, a player, by forcing an unnecessary delay between his opponent's first and second service, can disrupt a menacing rhythm. If a player's first service is faulty, his antagonist can pretend to tie up his shoe lace or otherwise make some delaying gesture to force discontinuity into his opponent's play. In cricket, similar circumstances occur. A batsman, by pretending to pat down an imaginary mound, can disturb the bowler's rhythm and put him off the game. A frustrated and impatient bowler is an erratic one. (Cohen, 1975)

Part of the reason for our ignorance about the issues raised must be attributed to the limited application of psychology to sporting behaviour and further to the limited scope of the models which have been adopted in the past. A hint of future developmental possibilities comes from the work of Kietliński (1975) who, in a paper which is critical of the overly mechanistic nature of many of the earlier models of decision-making, puts forward a revised model "for an integration of the basic dimensions of the decision situation" which he bases in part on a psychological analysis of the problem and part on his own intuitions. He makes the assumption that the person in a decision-making situation – confronted say, with two possible outcomes (positive or negative) – perceives and assesses the degree of risk (R) involved and then compares this estimate with the value to be gained V_g. If the trade-off R and V_g is favourable, this determines his decision. The interpretation of decision-making in terms of both perceived risk and gain seems intuitively sensible. Although no direct evidence is available in this respect from the sport psychology literature, it is not difficult to envisage the way in which risk and gain might be weighed, dependent upon the stage reached in, say, an important competitive match, the present standing of a team within a league or in situations which are potentially physically harmful to the person.

Cohen (1975) illustrates how the *image* of an opposing team might affect a contest:

> At the cup final in 1973, Leeds, by all reckoning, should have trounced Sunderland. But Leeds, near the top of the First division, may have been on edge. Confronting an 'inferior' team could have an inhibitory or confusing effect. Sunderland, by contrast, had everything to gain and not nearly so much to lose.

Certainly, tactical decisions about defensive or attacking play are generally based upon these two parameters. It is also well appreciated that there may be differences in opinion between spectator and player as to the merit of some decisions! While in part, this arises because the spectator does not know what is going on in the player's mind or because he is able to take a more detached view since he is involved in a different way, there are also other interesting reasons. One of the advantages of watching a sporting competition from on high or via television is not only that one gets a less interrupted view, but also one is able to examine the pattern of the game from a more advantageous position. The spectator so placed has access to information not available to the player. He may observe that the player's decision is a bad one but fail to appreciate that on the basis of the information available to the player, i.e. from his point of view, the decision was a logical one. It is significant in this respect that coaches of American football will often observe a game from a high spot in the stand, relaying such information to a second coach on the touchline. The importance of both perceived risk and pay-off assessment and their balancing may also account for the well-known paradox that individual athletes or teams may do better against superior than against equal opposition (Cohen, 1975).

It is unfortunate that empirical evidence directed at some of these issues is not available. Possibilities can however be gauged by considering further the laboratory experiments carried out by Kietliński to test the model of risky decision-making – introduced earlier – which, in as far as it utilizes a physical skill, has implications for sports situations. The methodology is not unlike that of the earlier Cohen and Dearnaley (1962) study on footballers although the task in his experiment was dart-throwing at a target. After an acclimatization period in the situation, subjects were asked to give their subjective probability of hitting marks of different sizes from different distances. Such a procedure enabled the establishment of a base-line spread of subjective probability scores – from the most to the least favourable – of 0.837, 0.672, 0.514, 0.346 and 0.138 (designated A, B, C, D, E and F respectively).

Players were then presented with a series of 72 different gambles which consisted of one of the above (A–E) probability values (game conditions), the amount to lose (V_1) in case of a miss and amount to gain (V_a) in case of a hit (arbitrary monetary figures were assigned) as indicated in Table 4. Using a mathematically

Table 4 Excerpt from the list of proposed gambles

Gamble/ game number	*Subjective probability score and (condition)*	*Monetary units to be lost on miss*	*Monetary units to be gained on hit*	*Players' decision*
.	.	.	.	
.	.	.	.	
13	0.364 (D)	5	10	
14	0.514 (C)	10	50	
15	0.672 (B)	20	5	
16	0.837 (A)	50	20	
.	.	.	.	
.	.	.	.	

derived regression equation based on the proposed model, Kietliński[3] was able to predict with considerable accuracy the risk performance of subjects in the experiment. These predictions together with the *actual* percentage of subjects accepting a given gamble are illustrated in Figure 2. This, together with a calculated correlation coefficient of 0.873, gives support to the explanatory value of the model. Kietliński draws attention to some of the limitations implicit in the methodology utilized, and he further points out that:

> The solution, expressed in terms of a mathematical function, is constrained in many ways, and is to be regarded as an exemplification of the model and the research method.

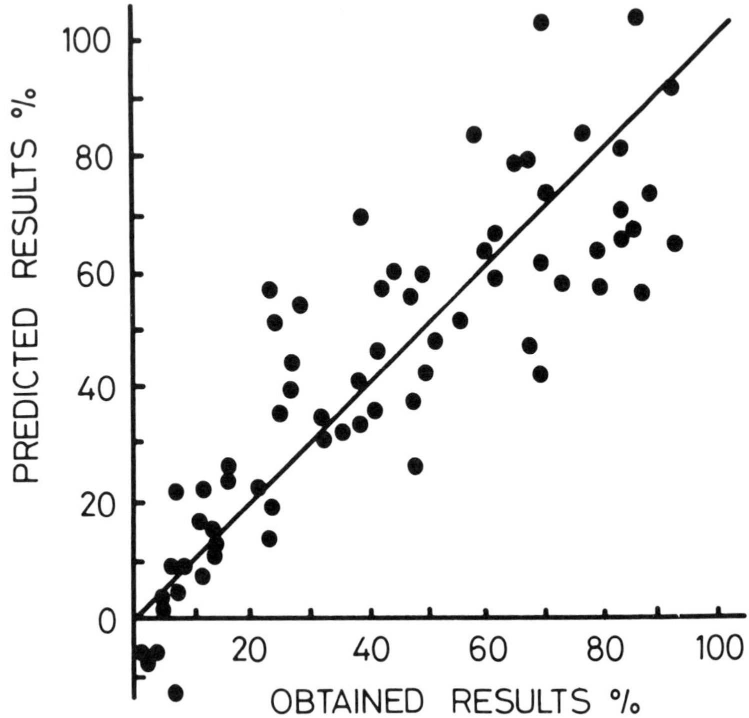

Figure 2 Interdependency of actual and predicted decisions, in percentages, to accept a game-play

SUBJECTIVE FATIGUE

The concept of physical fatigue has not unnaturally received considerable attention from sports psychologists, although the interpretations of the findings have been anything but consistent. In evaluating the traditional interpretations of fatigue in athletes, Blitz and van Moorst (1977) focus attention on their limited explanatory value particularly in as far as they look at 'changes in performance (output) as a result, *as well as* an indication of fatigue' and which overly pay attention to 'physiological parameters which are supposed to determine feelings of fatigue?' A more recent attempt to overcome these difficulties – they point out – is the rating of *subjective perception* of fatigue (Hueting, 1968) or exertion (Borg, 1962;

1972) which considers fatigue as a *perception* rather than a state. While Blitz and van Moorst appreciate the possibilities in this kind of interpretation, they are also cognizant of the difficulty raised by Taylor (1967) and previously referred to:

> The experimenter is not able directly to measure this assessment by the observer.

and as Blitz and van Moorst state:

> . . . it is unknown what the subjects are referring to: one can conceive the ratings as an estimation of load, of time (how long can I endure this), of exertion (effort), of pain or a mixture of all of these.

Blitz and van Moorst used a signal detection paradigm to examine some of the factors which relate to the perception of fatigue. While realizing – for reasons already discussed – that a signal detection model approach will not in itself provide a total explanation of the phenomenon, they were able to demonstrate its usefulness in assessing a related parameter – perception of differences in *load*. The isolation of this parameter was based on their contention that only work load (over time) remains as a valid factor in relation to perceived fatigue or exertion:

> This observation can be considered as a general conclusion: the seemingly trivial relation between work load and subjective perception of fatigue is the only one that stands to reason.

Utilizing a bicycle ergometer task under five different basic loads, and a signal detection paradigm, they were indeed able to demonstrate a relative increasing sensitivity over increasing work loads. Under extreme physiological fatigue, however, the discrimination deteriorated markedly, as indeed was demonstrated by Brooke, Hamley and Stone (1972) in a similar experiment in which the dependent variable was the detection of changes in air pressure applied to time-trial racing cyclists through a sphygmomanometer cuff resting distally against the medial malleolus projection.

ACHIEVEMENT MOTIVATION

While level of performance and hence victory or defeat are closely related to the skill level of the performer, Cohen's (1975) previous suggestion of the importance of 'confidence and the will to win' must not be underestimated, and must be taken into account in any comprehensive psychological model. While such parameters are difficult to operationalize, the subject of motivation and performance has occupied the attention of diverse groups of psychologists. The construct *achievement motivation*, coined by Atkinson (1964) to account for some of the variance between people involved in task situations which involve striving to reach perfection in performance, is of particular interest although the *generality* of such a concept has been questioned. Broverman, Jordan and Phillips (1960), for example, showed an inverse relationship between day-to-day achievement, striving and achievement in a specific environment, such as sport. In Usher's (1975) terms:

> Essentially they are saying that persons who are blocked in expressing achievement motivation in 'real-life' might be expected to show a great deal of striving on a task which might be more relevant for them.

In the present context, the importance of the construct relates to the fact that achievement situations involve choice under conditions of uncertainty. Thus, the person is faced with deciding amongst a number of alternative courses of action whose probability of success (*Ps*) is dependent upon what has been termed their *incentive value*. An earlier experiment[4] of Litwin (1958), for example, required players to participate in a game which involved tossing a ring over a peg from different distances (up to a maximum of 15 ft – 4.57 m) – which they had to determine subjectively. As well as actually performing on the task, players were required to state how much money up to a maximum of $1.00 they would allocate as a prize for a successful throw from a range of distances. The results are summarized in Table 5. The *subjective probability* of success (*Ps*) was obtained by requiring players to estimate how many times out of a hundred an *average* player from each range of distances would achieve success. The results compare favourably with the actual

Table 5 Theoretical and actual attractiveness of tasks of different difficulty in a ring toss game

Distances of throwing lines from target[a]	Value[b]		Probability of success (*Ps*)		Incentive value[c]		Proportion
	Prize money (cents)	*Task difficulty* ($1-Ps$)	*Perceived*	*Actual*	*Prize money* $\times Ps$	*Task difficulty* $\times Ps$	*Actual choice in 400 plays*
1–3	4	0.01	0.99		0.04	0.01	0.00
4–6	14	0.12	0.88	0.70	0.12	0.11	0.05
7–9	29	0.30	0.70	0.31	0.20	0.21	0.09
10–12	50	0.45	0.55	0.20	0.27	0.25	0.33
13–15	62	0.62	0.38	0.15	0.24	0.24	0.34
16–18	81	0.75	0.25	0.14	0.20	0.19	0.18

[a] Lines started at 10 inches (25.4 cm) from the target peg and subsequent lines were 10 inches (25.4 cm) apart to a maximum distance of 15 ft (4.57 m).

[b] Value was rated in terms of *either* money *or* difficulty.

[c] Incentive value (predicted attractiveness) was reasoned to be the product of expectancy (subjective probability of success) and value (in terms of money *or* difficulty).

achievement, as was demonstrated in the previous experiments discussed. *Incentive value* (predicted attractiveness) was reasoned to be a joint function of subjective probability of success (expectancy) and value (in terms of money *or* difficulty). Major incentive value was predicted to be for throwing distances lying between 10 and 15 ft (3.05 and 4.57 m), i.e. a medium level of difficulty. This was matched by the choices the players actually made over 400 throws at each distance.

Atkinson and Litwin (1960) in further experiments using a similar task also classified players as being high or low in achievement motivation. Players with high achievement motivation scores were shown to choose moderately difficult tasks (10–15 ft; 3.05–4.57 m) significantly more often than those with low achievement motivation scores.

Although the relationship between achievement motivation and success is unclear, it is generally assumed that high levels of performance are not achieved by people scoring low on achievement motivation measures. It is therefore not surprising that the achievement motivation of the athlete has received attention from sports psychologists. Cratty (1975), for example, maintains that extraordinary high needs for achievement are characteristic of the world-class athlete although, as Rushall (1970) points out, such a simplistic interpretation requires elaboration. In some instances there has been circularity of reasoning with level of achievement motivation being inferred from actual achievement.

Usher (1975), in a study of achievement motivation amongst various levels of football competitor, draws attention to the need to develop sport-specific items whose sensitivity to achievement motivation in a sport environment might be enhanced. In addition, he points the need to consider alternative incentive systems that may be operating for the athlete. Using four questionnaires (Costello, 1967) designed to obtain measures of:

1. the need to do well at a task (GN)
2. the need to be a success (GS)
3. the need to do well at a task specific to soccer (TSS)
4. the need to be a success specific to soccer (SSS)

administered to three ability groups of footballers (National, Provincial and Club) he was only able to demonstrate significant differences on the GN scores and the TSS scores. Both Provincial and Club groups had significantly higher levels of achievement motivation (need to do well at a task) than the National group. The Provincial group had significantly higher levels of achievement motivation specific to soccer than both the National and Club groups. Amongst the alternative explanations for the former finding, Usher suggests, is that contrary to previous findings (e.g. Cratty, 1975; Ogilvie, 1967) a high level of achievement motivation is not necessary to attain a high level of performance. Usher proposes that the lower scores of the National group on the TSS can be attributed to a shift from 'instrumental' to 'consummatory' behaviour:

> . . . having obtained a position on the National team the members have achieved their goal, and hence are no further motivated to strive intensely to perform well.

Some of the problems of interpretation arising from Usher's study may – as he hints – be due to problems with Atkinson's (1964) theory. Certainly, there has been questioning of some of its basic tenets by Boski (1975).

The findings of Boski's study suggest that, in diagnostic tasks at least, subjective probability and the incentive value of success (contrary to what might be expected from Atkinson's theory) are uncorrelated variables. Further, persons with a positive achievement motivation pattern do not tend to adopt a moderate assessment of their probability of success (*Ps*), incentive value of success (*Is*) or risk level when making decisions – again, contrary to Atkinson's theory. While these findings may be specific to tasks of a diagnostic nature, Boski maintains that his evidence is also critical of the more 'traditional' sphere of achievement-oriented behaviour. He also proposes – perhaps supporting Usher – that Atkinson's theory has failed to come to terms with differences in the interdependency of achievement motivation and elements of the decision situation in conditions of static and dynamic tasks, and in choice of task and final decision.

One final point over which Boski takes issue with Atkinson's theory, is the precise definition of 'risk' which he suggests is lacking:

> . . . in fact, risk is considered in contexts where it might be used interchangeably with subjective probability or even with level of

task difficulty. Thus we are faced with a notion of risk as a function of one element of the decision situation.

CONCLUDING REMARKS

This brief sortie into the field of subjective probability in sport has served to open a few avenues for possible development. It is clear from even such a brief overview that the concept is an important one for sports psychologists to consider when attention is focused on the decision processes of sports participants. To date, it is a concept which has been largely unexplored in this context. The reasons for this cannot easily be isolated. In part, they reflect the limited attention paid by psychologists to the applied field of sport and in part to the methodological difficulties implicit in relating the concept to such ecologically valid situations. Perhaps a chapter such as this will serve to remind those interested in sports psychology that it might prove a profitable field for further enquiry.

NOTES

1. Grateful acknowledgment is expressed to the authors and editor of the *British Journal of Psychology* for permission to adapt and reproduce a table and figure from Cohen, J. and Dearnaley, E. J. (1962).
2. Grateful acknowledgment is expressed to the authors and publishers, Messrs. Oliver and Boyd (Edinburgh) Ltd., for permission to adapt and reproduce a table from Cohen, J. and Christensen, I. P. (1970).
3. Grateful acknowledgment is expressed to the author and editor of the *Polish Psychological Bulletin* for permission to adapt and reproduce a table and figure from Kietliński, R. (1975).
4. Grateful acknowledgment is expressed to the publishers, General Learning Press, New Jersey, for permission to adapt and reproduce a table from McClelland, D. C. (1971).

BIBLIOGRAPHY

Atkinson, J. W. and Litwin, G. H. (1960). Achievement motive and test anxiety conceived as motive to approach success and motive to avoid failure. *Journal of Abnormal and Social Psychology*, **60**, 52–63

Atkinson, J. W. (1964). *An Introduction to Motivation*. (New York: Van Nostrand).

Blitz, P. S. and van Moorst, A. (1977). Physical fatigue and the perception of differences in load; a signal detection approach. Unpublished paper. Experimental Psychology Department, University of Amsterdam

Borg, G. (1962). *Physical Performance and Perceived Exertion*. (Lund: Gleerup).

Borg, G. (1972). The basis 'noise constant' in the psychophysical function of perceived exertion. Reports from the Institute of Applied Psychology, University of Stockholm

Boski, P. (1975). Motivational determinants of the diagnostic process. *Polish Psychological Bulletin*, **6**, 157–166

Broadbent, D. E. (1965). Applications of information theory and decision-theory to human performance and reaction. In: N. Wiener and J. P. Schade (eds.) *Progress in Brain Research*. (Amsterdam: Elsevier)

Broadbent, D. E. (1971). *Decision and Stress*. (London: Academic Press)

Brooke, J. D., Hamley, E. J. and Stone, P. T. (1972). Disturbances of attention and metabolic homeostasis during the performance of an exhausting physical activity. In: H. T. A. Whiting (ed.) *Readings in Sports Psychology*. (London: Henry Kimpton)

Broverman, D. W., Jordan, E. J. and Phillips, L. (1960). Achievement motivation in fantasy and behaviour. *Journal of Abnormal and Social Psychology*, **60**, 374–378

Cohen, J. (1957). *Subjective Probability*. Scientific American (reprint), November

Cohen, J. and Dearnaley, E.J. (1962). Skill and judgement of footballers in attempting to score goals. *British Journal of Psychology*, **53**, 71–88

Cohen, J. and Christensen, I. P. (1970). *Information and Choice*. (Edinburgh: Oliver and Boyd)

Cohen, J. (1975). Psychological aspects of sport with particular reference to variation in performance. In: H. T. A. Whiting (ed.) *Readings in Sports Psychology – 2*. (London: Lepus)

Coombs, C. H., Dawes, R. M. and Tversky, A. (1970). *Mathematical Psychology: An Elementary Introduction*. (New Jersey: Prentice-Hall)

Costello, C. G. (1967). Two scales to measure achievement motivation. *The Journal of Psychology*, **66**, 231–235

Cratty, B. J. (1975). *Psychology in Contemporary Sport*. (New Jersey: Prentice-Hall)

Edwards, W., Lindman, H. and Phillips, L. D. (1965). Emerging technologies for making decisions. In: *New Directions in Psychology*, Vol. II (New York: Holt, Rinehart and Winston)

Gallwey, W. T. (1974). *The Inner Game of Tennis*. (New York: Random House)

Hueting, J. W. (1968). *Psychofysiologisch Onderzoek van Lichamelijke Arbeid (Academisch Proefschrift)*. (Asten: Schriks' Drukkerij N.V.)

Kietliński, R. (1975). An empirical model of risky decisions. *Polish Pychological Bulletin*, **6**, 123–131

Knapp, B. (1964). *Skill in Sport*. (London: Routledge and Kegan Paul)

Kozielecki, J. (1975). The internal representation of risky tasks. *Polish Psychological Bulletin*, **6**, 115–121

Litwin, G. H.(1958). Motives and expectancy as determinants of preference for degrees of risk. Unpublished B.A. thesis, University of Michigan

Meredith, G. P. (1966). *Instruments of Communication*. (London: Pergamon)

Neisser, U. (1976). *Cognition and Reality*. (San Francisco: Freeman)

Ogilvie, B. C. (1967). What is an athlete? *Journal of Health, Physical Education and Recreation*, **38,** 48

Polanyi, M. (1958). *Personal Knowledge: Towards a Post-critical Philosophy*. (London: Routledge and Kegan Paul)

Poulton, E. C. (1950). Anticipation in open and closed sensori-motor skills. Unpublished paper, Medical Research Council's Applied Psychology Unit, Cambridge

Ricoeur, P. (1966). *Freedom and Nature: The Voluntary and the Involuntary*. (Northwestern University Press)

Robinson, G.H. (1964). Continuous estimation of a time-varying probability. *Ergonomics*, **7,** 7–23

Rushall, B. S. (1970). An investigation of the relationship between personality variables and performances categories in swimmers. *International Journal of Sports Psychology*, **1,** 2

Sharp, R.H. and Whiting, H. T. A. (1975). Information-processing and eye-movement behaviour in a ball-catching task. *Journal of Human Movement Studies*, **1,** 124–131

Shuford, E. H. (1971).Percentage estimation of proportion as a function of element type, exposure time, and task. *Journal of Experimental Psychology*, **61,** 430–436

Taylor, M. M. (1967). Detectability theory and the interpretation of vigilance data. In: A. T. Sanders (ed.) *Attention and Performance*. (Amsterdam: North Holland Publishing Co.)

Tyldesley, D. T. (1978). Timing in motor skills. Unpublished PhD thesis, University of Leeds

Usher, P. M. (1975). *Achievement motivation and levels of sport performance*. Movement, Actes du 7e Symposium en Apprentissage Pychomoteur et Psychologie du Sport, Octobre

Whiting, H. T. A. (1969). *Acquiring Ball Skill – A Psychological Interpretation*. (London: Bell)

Whiting, H. T. A. (1975). *Concepts in Skill Learning*. (London: Lepus)

Whitfield, D. (1967). Human skill as a determinant of allocation of function. In: W. J. Singleton, R. S. Easterby and D. C. Whitfield (eds.) *The Human Operator in Complex Systems*. (London: Taylor and Francis)

Wilberg, R. B. (1975). An analysis and application of game and human performance theory to sport and competition. In H. T. A. Whiting (ed.) *Readings in Sport Psychology*–2. (London: Lepus)

Williams, D. I. (1977). Psychobikistics. *Bulletin of the British Psychological Society*, **30,** 106–107

11

Levels of Uncertainty and Health Actions

LEO BARIC

The aim of this chapter is to outline a new approach to health education as the 'action' aspect of preventive medicine, based on the application of behavioural and social sciences in medicine. There are two distinguishable approaches to prevention of diseases due to people's behaviour and dependent on people's actions: the one treats individuals as 'rational' beings and concentrates on the most effective transmission of medical knowledge in the hope that people will assess rightly their probability of being at risk, make rational decisions based on appropriate and recommended choices, resulting in changes of their behaviour or specific actions, thus reducing the risk from a health threat; the other is based on the assumption that people's behaviour and actions are a consequence of the synergistic effects of the interaction of two factors – personal and social. The new approach in health education subscribes to the latter, postulating that to influence behaviour it is more economical to modify and influence social norms and utilize other social processes such as socialization than to change people's personal characteristics or influence their decisions and choices.

This societal approach in health education is directly related to Cohen's work on behaviour in uncertainty and his exploration of psychological as compared to mathematical probability. The change of emphasis from a psychological to a sociological treatment of problems related to influencing people's behaviour and actions is justified by Cohen's exposition of the complexity and variety of possible outcomes of individual actions which could not possibly all be covered by a health education intervention. Creating and modifying social expectations seems to be the only reasonable approach at the disposal of a population-oriented health education which promises certain success.

BEHAVIOUR–ACTION

There are many diseases that have been found to be related to human behaviour or dependent on a human action, so that we can today speak of 'behavioural medicine' (Burton, 1969). A certain pattern of diet can result in undernourishment or even rickets; a timely recognition of a lump in the breast as a serious symptom may result in timely seeking of medical advice and reduce considerably the adverse outcome. In the former case we talk about behaviour and in the latter about an action, which may be defined as behaviour that is just not a response but has a specific meaning or intention (Weber, 1947).

The behaviour–action continuum (Figure 1) illustrates a set of processes and influences derived from institutionalized or new knowledge about illness and health threats. Institutionalized knowledge is reflected in social expectations or norms about the preservation of health and the prevention and cure of illness. These norms are internalized by individuals as routines or habits, and become a part of the role performance that accompanies a specific social position or status. New knowledge reaches the individual either as a part of new or modified norms or as a set of new alternative choices which may form the basis for a decision about the preservation of health and prevention or cure of a disease.

There are many examples of institutionalized knowledge about health and illness being transmitted as a part of the socialization process and resulting in routines or habits of the recipient. Most of the hygienic habits of cleanliness, avoidance of accidents, preference for specific foods prepared in a specific way, the exercise–rest sequence, etc., are internalized by a child during the process of primary socialization as routines and habits to be carried out throughout his adult life. This institutionalized knowledge, reflected in social expectations or norms, reinforces routines and habits that form a part of health-related behaviour serving to maintain health and prevent disease. Institutionalized knowledge is, however, undergoing constant changes due to the incorporation of new discoveries in the medical field. These discoveries either modify the existing norms or create new ones. The discovery of the importance of fluoride in the preservation of dental health modified the existing routine of tooth-brushing by

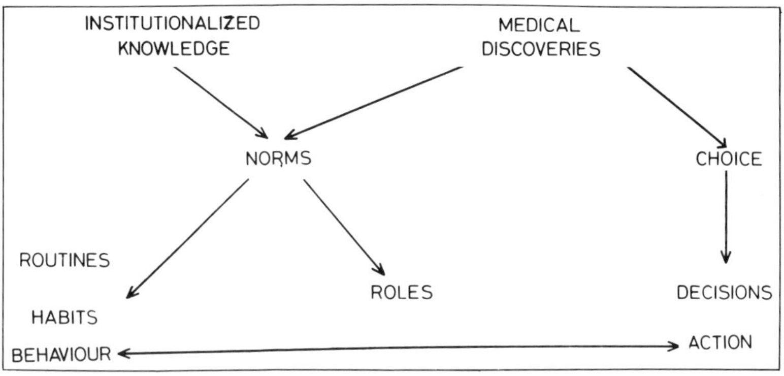

Figure 1 A set of processes and influences derived from institutionalized or new knowledge about illness in relation to the behaviour–action continuum

introducing this substance into toothpaste or water, or as tablets to be taken by children. The discovery of the dangers of overweight in early childhood for the health of children when they grow up brought about a new norm concerning our image of a healthy baby and changed our emphasis on weighing of babies and equating a fat with a 'bonny' baby.

Institutionalized knowledge, updated and modified by new medical discoveries, is also reflected in norms concerning a person's role-performance according to a recognized social position or status (Baric, 1969). Disease represents a social as well as personal dysfunction. To minimize and regulate the disruptive consequences, such dysfunctions are integrated into the social structure as specific statuses with appropriate roles. We can distinguish among the statuses of being healthy, ill or at risk. The difference between a state and a status is that the former represents a personal feeling and the latter a formally recognized social position, legitimized by formally recognized agents and accompanied by a set of rights and obligations. A person may feel well and go about his everyday business without giving a thought to his health and we would say that he is feeling 'healthy'. If, however, such a person wants to apply for a mortgage to buy a house and to take out an insurance policy, he would need a formal confirmation of his health state. By undergoing a medical examination, his doctor would be able to declare him healthy or to legitimize his status of being healthy with all the accompanying rights and duties. If a person attempts to start his car on a cold winter morning, he may find that his car battery is flat and he may attempt to do something about it, like cleaning the leads, recharging it, etc. As a result of handling the battery he will be in a state of risk from lead poisoning if he does not protect his hands or wash them before eating. On the other hand, a person may work in a garage or a car battery factory where such a risk from lead poisoning is formally recognized and legitimized by allocating to that person a status of being at risk. He will have certain rights such as regular screening, possibly additional 'danger' money, etc., and certain obligations such as wearing protective clothing, not smoking at work, personal cleanliness, etc. Another person may feel headachy and have a sore throat when waking in the morning and he would be in a state of feeling unwell. If, however, he decides to stay at home he may need to have his state legitimized by his doctor who would, upon examination, allocate to him a status of being ill. He would then acquire the right not to go to work, to expect sympathy and consideration from his family, etc., and would be obliged to stay in bed, to take medicines and be in medical terms cooperative.

A person's role performance for each specific status is defined by a set of norms or formally recognized social expectations, and can consequently be classified as conformist or deviant (Baric, 1975). There is, however, usually a grey area where the performance does not quite match the expectations but is still within the limits of accepted tolerance and is classified as variant. The willingness of a person to acquire a status implies his willingness to conform to the norms defining his role behaviour. This willingness is influenced by the coercive power of a norm which is based on supportive sanctions. In other words, the acquisition of a status followed by deviant behaviour will invoke sanctions imposed by the society.

The recognition of the societal aspects of different health states with matched statuses and roles has had a great impact on recent developments in health education. Because of the realization that health messages do not always produce the desired results, health educators have been considering other possible approaches. This has resulted in a critical assessment of the advantages of a societal approach compared with influencing personal choices (Baric, 1977).

DECISIONS ABOUT HEALTH ACTIONS

New insights into the causes of some health threats as a result of some medical discovery may take some time before they become integrated into institutionalized knowledge and formalized norms (Figure 1). In such a case the individual will find himself in a position of assessing the evidence, with a freedom of choice when deciding whether to undertake a specific action or not and without any threat of sanctions or other forms of social coercion.

The usual sequence of events has been that a research discovers a statistically significant association between a personal characteristic or behavioural pattern and the increased risk from a disease. This was the case when Doll and Hill (1950) substantiated the existing suspicion of an association between cigarette smoking and lung cancer. This triggered off a whole spate of research to support or disprove it, and became an issue of public concern. Some people used it for fund-raising purposes and the establishment of public associations, whereas others used it as a reason for starting numerous health education projects to stop people from smoking. The strong feelings of health educators about the desirability of the recommended behavioural change have not been matched by the willingness of the client-population to comply with the advice received. Because of this failure an enormous amount of money and effort has been spent in finding out why the majority of smokers do not give up the habit in the face of the evidence linking smoking to such a dreaded disease as cancer.

In his review of studies related to this problem, Dunn (1973) outlined the main approaches taken by the researchers in trying to find an answer to the question of how to make people stop smoking. Some researchers started from the assumption that there is a decisive difference between smokers and non-smokers in the hope that by comparing the two they would find the answer. Others decided that this is a waste of time and that one should go to the smokers directly and ask them why they smoke and, thus, from them get the answer to the problem. Yet another group of researchers believed that smoking is an addiction and tried to establish physiological changes induced by tobacco constituents, expecting to find a solution in this way. Each group of researchers mentioned came up with a whole set of associations of scientific interest but no practical value for health education.

Health education has been so far mainly engaged in transmitting to people information about new discoveries related to the prevention of diseases together with the recommended measures for the reduction of the attached risk. So far it has had relatively little success in spite of the obvious logic of the arguments used. New insight into this problem has been gained by studies of decision-making and of choice between several existing alternatives.

An important contribution to the understanding of these problems has been made by Cohen (1972). It provided an insight into the assessment of the subjective or 'psychological' probability attached to statistical evidence about a health threat as perceived by an individual when confronted with a health education message recommending a behavioural change. It also contributed to the understanding of problems related to receiving, understanding and acting upon a message received by the introduction of the concept of thresholds: the information threshold, the psychological probability threshold and the action threshold.

The information threshold

The first question to be faced is what kind of and how much information a person must receive before even starting to relate it to himself and start assessing the utility of the recommended change against the disutility of the discomfort accompanying such a step.

It is a well-known fact that knowledge as such is not in most cases sufficient to initiate the desired action. A study concerning the influence of knowledge about the stages of the development of a fetus *in utero* on the opinion whether and when an abortion should be legally allowed (Baric and Harrison, 1977) showed that there was no direct relationship between the two. Even when health education as a part of the study was carried out and subjects' knowledge was increased, no change in the respondents' opinion was observed.

This was also confirmed in a study of smoking habits, comparing medical with non-medical students (Baric, MacArthur and Fisher, 1976). In addition to knowledge, the study also explored the relationship between students' attitudes to smoking and their actual smoking behaviour. There was no significant difference in smoking between the two groups, although the medics had a higher level of knowledge and fewer positive attitudes to smoking.

Following the interpretations given by Cohen (1972), various people would appear to need different amounts of information before they reach their information threshold. Some may, however, make their decision 'instantaneously' as Fellner and Marshall (1970) found when investigating the response to an appeal for kidney donors; 14 out of 20 donors reported making their decision 'in a split second'. In other cases more information may be needed, or information with certain 'weight' before the threshold is reached.

Psychological probability threshold

Once the information threshold has been passed, a person will start to assess the possibility and the probability of a threat affecting him and what the consequences might be. Cohen (1964) has drawn a clear distinction between the objective or mathematical probability of an event's occurring and the subjective or psychological probability a person gives to that event. This problem has been largely neglected in health educational studies and Cohen's work in this area represents a major contribution to health education. Most health education activities have been and still are limited to the transmission of information in the hope that people, as 'rational' beings, will heed the advice. Since this does not always follow, an insight into personal interpretation of information about a risk to health is very important.

One of the clues to the way people assess information about a probable risk to their health can be derived from the description Cohen gives of a person's translation of a population probability to his own personal (or sample) probability. According to probability theory, this cannot be done, since by definition a population probability can never be attributed to any specific event or individual in that population. We can say that the probability of a positive smear in a cervical cancer screening test is 7 in 1000 but we cannot say which seven it will be in that population or even how many thousands of women must be screened before we get this level of probability. And yet, this is exactly the argument used in many health education programmes to influence individual women to come for a test. This is based on empirical evidence that people daily try to guess what their chances are, when deciding about an action.

How do people make such interpretations, and could the understanding of this process help health education? Cohen gives a very plausible explanation in describing a trial of children at different ages given the task of guessing the number of yellow and blue beads in an array of beakers from the information about the whole population of beads. The guesses were not solely dependent on information about the population but were governed by people's ideas about the population (macrocosm), which they then translate to apply to themselves (microcosm). These ideas can be coloured by different influences such as ethical and aesthetical beliefs as well as by one's own image. One can overestimate the probability of something that is considered to be beautiful or good, or if one is an optimist.

The translation of a person's image about the macrocosm in interpreting the events concerning his microcosm has also been described by Suchman (1969), although in a different context. He related people's behaviour to their orientation to health care system. Suchman described two distinctive types of orientation: parochial and cosmopolitan. People with a parochial orientation showed a low level of medical knowledge; their knowledge was based on popular beliefs and personal experiences, and was acquired through informal sources; in illness they showed a high level of dependence on their immediate social environment (family and friends): they also showed a high level of scepticism about medical care system and its agents. The cosmopolitans showed a high level of medical knowledge based on scientific evidence and acquired through formal sources such as the educational system or scientific literature; in illness they showed a low level of dependence on family and friends, and they were not at all sceptical about the health care system or their agents. When health education information is transmitted through public channels and bases its arguments on scientific concepts such as probability, the cosmopolitans are more likely to accept it than the parochials. This has been supported by studies of utilization of health services and modification of behaviour.

Lack of willingness to accept the arguments presented by health educators in favour of a change in behaviour may also be due to the misinterpretations of the probabilistic statements made. People in general have difficulties in differentiating between the 'possibility' and the 'probability' of an event occurring. This may be because it is usual for people to reason that something may or may not happen, i.e. that they will become ill or will stay well. This 'either–or' approach is treated as a 50 : 50 probability. The fallacy, however, is that these two events need not be equiprobable. The realistic interpretation would be, that although they can become ill or not, if they smoke their chance of becoming ill is twenty times higher than for non-smokers.

Another common fallacy is to treat discrete events as a sequence of events instead of each one separately. When told that smoking in pregnancy may harm the fetus (Baric and MacArthur, 1977), women who had smoked during their previous pregnancy and had a healthy baby in general disregarded such information. They believed that since it did not happen before, it 'cannot' happen now. On the other hand, it is known that parents with one mongol baby find it very difficult to believe that the next one will not be a mongol too.

An interesting story was reported in *The Times* (23.9.1977) from Bucharest, about an air crash in which the aircraft was split in two and half of the passengers were killed. A survivor from Turkey in describing the accident concluded "Having survived the accident I think I am now 'insured' against tragic happenings like this and won't be fatally involved in other aircraft crashes. I travel a lot by air". In Cohen's terms, the person must have obviously been an optimist, since if he had been a pessimist he could have equally logically reasoned, that since he survived one crash, in the next one he would most certainly be killed.

The action threshold

Whether a person will undertake an action, after passing through the information- and psychological probability-thresholds, will also depend on passing through the action-threshold. Even then it will still not be certain what kind of action will follow.

The first question, therefore, will be what makes a person undertake an action? Becker (1974) in his review lists a number of models applied by various researchers in an attempt to find this answer. A popular and probably most widely used model in health education has been the Health Belief Model described by Rosenstock (1974). It postulates that a health action depends on a person's belief in his own susceptibility to the health threat; that the occurrence of that disease would at least have a moderate severity on some component of his life; and that taking some action would in fact be beneficial by reducing his susceptibility to the condition, or if the disease did occur, by reducing its severity and that it would not entail overcoming important psychological barriers such as cost, pain, convenience and embarrassment. This model has been used in a number of retrospective, prospective and intervention studies and was found to be of descriptive value rather than predictive. Later an additional factor was included, i.e. a 'cue', which seems to be most important in triggering off an action even if all the other factors are present. There have been several criticisms of this model: it does not include motivation as a factor; each person will provide his own cue if he decides to act; the factors in the model have not been standardized; they do not represent discrete units, etc.

Becker also discusses other models related to this problem (Lewin, Toeman, Rotter, Edwards, Atkinson and Feather) some of which employ the notion of behaviour in uncertainty and psychological probability related to making a choice. It seems, however, that the complete understanding of the psychological mechanisms which prompt a person to undertake an action still eludes us, and that each of the models mentioned explains only a part of the process without providing a complete answer.

Once a decision has been made and an action follows, we are faced with the problem of what kind of action it will be. An intervention study carried out among pregnant women (Baric, MacArthur and Sherwood, 1976) with the aim of informing them about the dangers of smoking during pregnancy illustrates this point. A doctor in an ante-natal clinic talked with a number of pregnant women about the dangers to their unborn child, in an attempt to persuade them to give up smoking during pregnancy. In an interview in their homes 11 weeks after the intervention it was found that 52% of the women had reacted and did undertake some action. Although all of them received the same kind of information, supported by similar kinds of arguments, the range of their reactions was considerable: 10% stopped smoking, 7% stopped but started again, 24% reduced and 11% increased the number of cigarettes smoked. The rest (48%) reported no change.

From all the studies cited, as well as from other literature, it seems obvious that the problem of making a decision which will result in a recommended action is much more complex than would appear from the existing models currently in use. It has also been shown that there is no such thing as a 'health action' or 'health behaviour', but that we are dealing with specific reactions of individuals to specific health threats or disease symptoms. One person may make up his mind 'instantaneously' when confronted with the facts, whereas another may need a long time and a vast amount of information before even considering the possibility of acting. One individual may react negatively to too little information about one health threat and also negatively to too much information about another threat. It is also known that a low level of perceived susceptibility may inhibit one kind of action (vaccination), whereas too high a level of perceived susceptibility may inhibit or delay some other action (breast examination).

IMPLICATIONS FOR HEALTH EDUCATION

Telling people what is best for them is not sufficient to reduce the prevalence in a population of a health threat due to behaviour. The examination of various attempts to find an effective way of achieving this reduction supports this assumption. It has been shown, following Cohen, that it is not theoretically correct to translate a population probability of a risk to its individual members. It has also been shown that, although individuals tend to do this all the time, the translation will depend on individual characteristics, value orientation, cultural and social background, etc. This indicates that it cannot be used as a practical tool for planning a health education approach aimed at individuals. It has been, furthermore, shown that individual perceptions of probability of a health threat differ to such an extent that no individual-based approach to a population could cover all the necessary variations. This has been supported by findings from mass health education campaigns, most of which have been effective only for a small proportion of a population. It should not be forgotten that nearly everybody in England knows about the risk smokers run from lung cancer and some other diseases, and yet only approximately 20% of smokers give it up in any one year. Even if smokers have attended some smoking clinic where more intensive methods are being used, only a similar percentage give it up for at least one year.

This brings us back to Figure 1, which shows various ways health knowledge is transmitted and internalized. It would appear (Baric, 1976) that the most economical procedure for health education would be to influence routines and habits through the socialization process and at the same time to institutionalize at-risk statuses with accompanying norms for each health threat. This is the way in which health education can operate successfully on a population level. Individuals who do not conform to social expectations (deviants) and other special cases can then be approached on an individual level by specially trained health educators and other professionals. In the case of new medical discoveries, it will also be more economical for health education to concentrate on the integration of this new knowledge into new norms with sufficient power to act as a cue for individual action. In this way people could conform to well-defined social expectations related to health instead of making haphazard individual choices which may produce unexpected and undesirable results.

BIBLIOGRAPHY

Baric, L. (1969). Recognition of the 'at-risk role': A means to influence health behaviour. *International Journal of Health Education*, **12,** 2–12

Baric, L. (1975). Conformity and deviance in health and illness. *International Journal of Health Education,* **18,** 1–12

Baric, L. (1976). Preparation of manpower for health education: a comparative view. *Health Education Monographs*, **4,** number 3

Baric, L. (1977). Social expectations *versus* personal preferences. *Journal of the Institute of Health Education*, **15**(3), 23–28

Baric, L. and Harrison, A. (1977). Social pressure and health education. *Journal of the Institute of Health Education*, **15**(4), 12–18

Baric, L. and MacArthur, C. (1977). Health norms in pregnancy. *British Journal of Preventive and Social Medicine,* **31,** 30–38

Baric, L., MacArthur, C. and Fisher, C. (1976). Norms, attitudes and smoking behaviour among Manchester students. *Health Education Journal*, **35,** 142–150

Baric, L., MacArthur, C. and Sherwood, M. (1976). A study of health educational aspects of smoking in pregnancy. *International Journal of Health Education,* **19,** 1–16

Becker, M. H. (ed.) (1974). The health belief model and personal health behaviour. *Health Education Monographs*, **2,** number 4

Burton, J. (1969). Health education in behavioural medicine. In: Hobson (ed.) *The Theory and Practice of Public Health.* (Oxford University Press)

Cohen, J. (1964). *Behaviour in Uncertainty.* (London: Allen and Unwin)

Cohen, J. (1972). *Psychological Probability or the Art of Doubt.* (London: Allen and Unwin)

Doll, R. and Hill, A. B. (1950) Smoking and the Carcinoma of the lung. *British Medical Journal,* **2,** 739

Dunn, W. L. (ed.) (1973). *Smoking Behaviour: Motives and Incentives.* (Washington: Winston)

Fellner, C. H. and Marshall, J. R. (1970). Kidney donors. In: J. Macauley and L. Berkowitz (eds.). *Altruistic and Helping Behaviour.* (London: Academic Press)

Rosenstock, T. M. (1974). Historical origins of the health belief model. In: H. M. Becker (ed.). The health belief model and personal health behaviour. *Health Education Monographs*, **2,** number 4

Suchman, E. A. (1969). Social factors in illness behaviour. *Milbank Memorial Fund Quarterly*, **47** (Part II), 85–93

Weber, M. (1947). *The Theory of Social and Economic Organisation.* (London: Macmillan)

12

The Theory of Conflict and the Concept of Probability

JOHAN GALTUNG

PROBABILITY AND UNCERTAINTY

In this essay some efforts will be made to explore the relationship between conflict and probability. Inevitably, something has to be said by way of introduction about these two key concepts – they are subject to a high number of interpretations, so some exploration of these concepts is a necessary condition if they are to be related to each other. However, the explorations will be simple and preliminary, an effort not to do more in that direction than what is needed to arrive at some more interesting interconnections.

To start with probability: it is the "degree of rational belief" expressed by Carnap[1] rather than "idealized relative frequency" of von Mises[2] that is most interesting for the present purpose. As a matter of fact, the word 'rational' is not even necessary. Nor are we concerned with measurement of subjective probability; it is actually the very idea of uncertainty that is important. That excludes two possibilities: the certainty that something will happen and the certainty that something will not happen.

In the whole range of uncertainty there is one particular point, or interval, that deserves some specific mention: the idea of 'perfect uncertainty'. We shall not identify it with 'equiprobability'; that gives to the symmetric rather than the asymmetric a much too fundamental position in epistemology[3]. But the concept 'perfect uncertainty' is a very tricky one. Thus, imagine that one is driving at full speed on the wrong side of a highway; what the outcome will be is not certain, it is 'uncertain'. But does that mean that the driver can tell himself: "50% I survive; 50% I die; hence I stand a fair chance of survival"? Of course not, that would be a very optimistic bet indeed. But why is this 'of course not'? Because we do possess *some* knowledge about what happens on highways – cars have a tendency to use them and the highways in turn have a tendency to be used; when used, cars have a tendency to drive on the correct side of the road and, given this, collisions may easily be produced if one insists on using the wrong lane. The highway *may* by some coincidence be empty that particular hour and/or only be used by cars that by some other coincidence might decide to use the wrong lane – but the chances are slim. Why? – presumably because we have been watching or participating in highway life and for that reason have built into us some kind of knowledge. Outcomes are not equiprobable; there is a bias. Somehow the notion of 'perfect uncertainty' should be evaluated relative to that bias – it does not mean that outcomes are equally likely; it must mean something else out of which the case of equiprobability is a special case.

Maybe the key to this lies in the word 'subjective' and 'belief'; and not in the word 'rational', at least not if narrowly interpreted. For why do people engage in some many actions about which outsiders might say that they certainly do not stand a fair chance of succeeding; even surviving? To take a political example of a very contemporary nature: why do South African whites in general, and their nationalist leadership in particular, persist in white supremacist rule? Why don't they see the 'handwriting on the wall', firmly written, usually by black hands – *your time is out*. Is it because they think: "50% we are out, 50% we will still be in"? Maybe it is fair to say that they do not *think* this, but they *wish* it to be true – in other words that the wish is the master of the thought to the extent that the situation *is* interpreted in terms of fair chances. How people persuade themselves in such cases is probably relatively simple: in general, in similar situations, ours would have been a hopeless case; *but in our case,* given our special situation, capacities, intentions, what is generally true no longer holds. In other words, there will be a tendency to reinterpret the situations to de-objectify them, to particularize rather than universalize, to build one's own little sample of one case drawn from one's own little universe. A human right, and need, indeed! – but not 'rational'.

And this may also be the case with a daredevil driver on the wrong side of the road: "what holds for ordinary people does not hold for me". And it may be the case for the criminal: he may be in the possession of perfect statistics about detection and conviction probabilities, yet feel that "this applies to ordinary people, not to me". In other words, our argument is that subjective probability can be interpreted as really subjective probability, not contaminated by precise or vague notions of relative frequencies, or some theory as to how the dice are loaded, even when they have not been thrown yet.

It may be objected that people are not that simple; they may have their wishes, but at the same time they may also have their empirically or theoretically inspired thoughts – indeed, wishes, data and theories do not come in three separate compartments. With this one should agree completely, and rather talk about separate types of consciousness. A person may at one layer know (in the relative frequency sense) that his chances are very slim, at another layer wish (in the subjective belief sense) that the chances are fair – one does not exclude the other. The psychology of their relationship is a complex one, and need not concern us here, except for one thing: if the chances 'objectively' speaking are slim, and the moment of truth is appearing, this will probably have an impact on the person psychodynamically that may cause the objective probability estimate to recede even further into the background and the subjective belief or faith to dominate the scene, thus inspiring the daredevils' courage. This is, it seems, the reason why people do the kinds of things they do in wars: diving their planes into enemy fire in order to drop a bomb or two, dashing out of the trenches in the face of mortal enemy fire, and so on – "It does not apply to me, it cannot apply to me, at least not here, at least not now!"

Let us now make use of these reflexions in order to come a step closer to conflict. Imagine that human beings were somehow different, that we were condemned to perfect certainty. In other words, we would know in advance the consequences of our action; the future would be as clear to us as the past. There would be no uncertainty, we would not only know the consequences of our choices, but also know our choices – meaning that they would no longer be choices. For anybody who belongs to the managerial (governmental and non-governmental, national or international) 'elites' of our overdeveloped societies it is well known what that means: it means that your calendar is so filled up one year in advance, that there is hardly any empty space where you can even *write* down the possibility of a week-end outing with your family, let alone doing it. The future is as predictable as future trains, the calendar has become like a railway itinerary – referring now to Swiss trains, not, for instance, to Southern Italian local trains or to British trains, steered by a strike-conditioned on-again–off-again pattern. Another comparison would be with prison life: utterly predictable, practically speaking all important choices have already been made for the prisoner, the spectrum of consequences is a narrow one, and fairly quickly known to the inmate.

Much can be said about this type of condition; let us only spell out some aspects. Thus, words like 'boredom', 'apathy' and the famous 'wish for new experience' (Thomas) will easily come to one's mind. But the implications are deeper than this sense of being programmed, or having been reduced to an automaton with no options left. There is also the perspective that the lifelines, the trajectories along which one will travel through future life, end at one point, with death. There is a tremendous qualitative difference between knowing in the abstract that sooner or later we shall all die and knowing concretely the when, where, how and why; to have it written into the diary at some future date, so to speak. In face of that certainty, specified with details – would we still go on living? In a sense the question is wrong because it is assumed that our knowledge is absolute and correct; if suicide were in our future we would already know it. Quite possibly it might not induce despair, but even relieve us of anxieties tied to uncertainties. It might be a happy automaton, but nonetheless an automaton.

However, in a sense equally importantly: would not human beings equipped with perfect certainty about the future also mean the end to human history? How could human beings under such conditions create history, meaning by that social transformation, transcendencies, new patterns of life? Could it be built into the certainty of the future that they would, in 22 years (the magic year 2000 that all future studies are now focusing on) lead different lives[4]? Would certainly about what is going to happen make them engage in the type of action that is a condition for something new to happen? Can human beings be programmed to transcend themselves? Or, will at least a great portion of what we refer to as 'transcendence' necessarily have to come out of *praxis*, an accumulation of social experience by venturing into the unknown?

THE CONCEPT OF CONFLICT

We shall now try to show by some examples that not only is uncertainty a necessary condition for what one might refer to as the historicity of human beings, it may also be said to be a necessary condition for human life itself. And to do this we shall make use of the concept of conflict.

The definition we shall use of conflict is as follows: it is the situation that obtains when *one or more actors are pursuing incompatible goals*. Thus, there are four key concepts: actors, pursuit, incompatibility and goals. Some remarks about all four:

As to actors

There may be only one actor and the conflict is an intra-actor conflict, or a so-called dilemma – e.g. relating to the person's distribution of activities through time and space (shall I spend my Saturday morning working or enjoying myself?) The actors may be individual or collective, the latter may be organized with hard nuclei called 'states' (that in turn have even harder nuclei called 'governments'), or they may be very loosely tied together in associations and organizations. But they all have one thing in common: there is a certain amount of crystallization, an awareness of goals, a mapping of strategies.

As to pursuit

The actors act, there is activity, there are efforts to do something – preferably to arrive at not only one goal state but also the others that might be competitive with it. Something is standing in the way, otherwise there would be no conflict and that thing standing in the way is by definition also the pursuit of a goal, by oneself or by others.

As to incompatibility

This is a tricky concept, subject to many subdivisions and interpretations. Some of the same distinctions, as for the theory of probability, enter here: between objective incompatibility and subjective incompatibility. On the one hand, if the actor or actors believe that certain goals are incompatible they might give up in advance, contenting themselves with one of the goals at the expense of the other (or some compromise, half-way consummation of either). But they might also push on, beyond their subjective beliefs, and encounter some hard resistances that might look to them like more objective obstacles. Conversely: they might bump into these obstacles before any subjective beliefs, based on experience, have been formed. Moreover, incompatibilities may obviously be more or less absolute. The hardest one to deal with may be logical rather than empirical. If A and B both want to dominate the other, there is perfect agreement between the two of them as to what is meant by domination and they want exactly the same type of domination in the same type of situation, then it is hard to see how both can obtain their goals: 'A dominates B' and 'B dominates A' seem to exclude each other rather neatly. This, however, is not the case with 'A rules Milano' and 'B rules Milano' – they might rule together, in a biconsular fashion. (More problematic if the goal states are 'A rules Milano alone' and 'B rules Milano alone' – unless they would be willing to say that 'alone' only means that *when* they rule, e.g. every second day, *then* they rule alone.)

As to goals

These are states of affairs wished for, desired, 'cathected'; what actors are striving for, at any given point in time and space. They are not the final state of affairs, they may be just intermediary stops on the road. Goals differ in many ways, one of them – and an important one – being the extent to which they can be gradually consumed (like an apple) or the consummation is an all-or-nothing affair (some of the examples above).

It should be noted that what has now been to some extent defined is a special case of a much broader category that could be referred to as 'social contradictions'. This would then define a spectrum where 'conflict' would be on one end, and on the other end would be parties rather than actors with interests rather than goals, ritualistically performing their social roles where the incompatibilities are not brought out into the open precisely because the parties are not conscious and crystallized enough to become actors and the interests have not, through a process of conscientization, been transformed into goals. The contradiction is there in a more latent sense, in the social reality as between parents and children – the parents wanting the children to be pettable, responsive rather than responsible, protected rather than protecting, able to reciprocate the tenderness bestowed upon them by the parents; whereas it might be in the children's interest as soon as possible to conquer platforms in adult life, such as the right to work (not the right to be exploited, though). The transformation from contradictions in general to crystallized conflicts is an important chapter in conflict theory.

One thesis might now be formulated as follows: human history is the history of contradictions that crystallize into conflicts, are acted out, resolved in various ways thereby transforming social reality; in this new reality new contradictions start building up, crystallize into conflicts that in turn are acted out, and so on and so forth. The process goes from infinity to infinity, it has no beginning and no end, it is inextricably linked to human life itself. But the condition for this to happen is that actors act, and one condition for them to act – it will be argued – is that they do not possess perfect certainty about the outcomes of the action. In fact, the absence of perfect certainty might possibly be said to be a characteristic of action as opposed to (ritualistic) behaviour.

In a sense the point is very simple. Take as an example the type of struggle that women all over the world are engaged in today, at various levels of consciousness and crystallization/mobilization. Take the point of departure as it has developed in the industrialized, western, capitalist countries: the family as a feudal/conservative enclave in a capitalist/liberal social formation in which the men participate fully, the women (and the children and the aged) only marginally, being more treated like serfs in those feudal enclaves by 'their' men. To say that they are treated as slaves is nonsense: they are not bought and sold, but they are tied to the setting, unfree to move, very limited rights of ownership or disposition of anything, legally inferior, etc. The fight for the right to divorce is the fight for the right to move from the fief, and (from a man's angle) the right to cut the obligations to maintain that particular fief. The family, like the feudal unit in earlier periods, is a set of reciprocal rights and duties, both ways, so there is always a double edge to all the arguments in this context – this is a reason why there is a complementarity, indeed a dialectic to the liberation of women and the liberation of men. For all this to happen, women have to become conscious, they have to mobilize, they have to fight with the various means at their disposal – an obvious one being to go on strike – to refuse to be the helpers preparing the men for participation in macro-society, to groom him when he comes home, wounded from real or imagined battles, to participate in 'his success'.

No doubt we are right now in the transformation phase of contradiction to clear crystallized conflict. But that immediately raises the agonizing question: what is the goal state? Is it the equal participation of women on a 50% basis, in all positions in capitalist/liberal social formations, whether the capitalism is of the private or state varieties? Is 50% women in CIA and KGB a goal worth fighting for? – Is the effort to throw doubt on this goal a clever male strategy to keep women in their place, as serfs? As the conflict proceeds through various types of conflict dynamics such positions will increasingly be conquered; the goal comes closer. The fight has been guided by a vision, a dream – words like 'equity' and 'social justice' have dominated that dream. As one comes closer the dream fades, the goal recedes; as one mountain is being scaled it not only appears less golden than it looked at a distance, other mountains appear on the horizon behind the first one. On such mountains other goals may be written: 'equal participation', yes, but in a different social formation – perhaps – after all – more similar to the family than to the enormous macro-societies that have emerged since the Middle Ages. No doubt as one moves closer to that mountain it will also appear less golden and there will also appear new mountains on the horizon behind that one again, and so on and so forth.

What makes us do all this? Think of the workers who started early last century or the women who started early this century; think of the odds against them! Any kind of knowledge based on relative frequencies would tell them very clearly what the position of workers and women was; the positivistic attitude carried by the relative frequency interpretation of probability gives to the past a very loud voice, to the future only the promise of stochastic convergence towards the idealized relative frequency, the 'probability'. A very meagre promise indeed, not much material for a dream – except for those who belong to the privileged groups, the elites, largely staffed by MAMUs (Middle-Aged Men with University education). Think of the odds that are against other groups in the same position when they will start the same fight, marching on the same long road: the old-age home inmates, the pensioners and retired people in general, the children, the very young, the non-intellectuals in an intellectualizing society. If their guidelines were based on knowledge extracted from the past alone inaction would be the rational consequence and those who would want this type of consequence to be drawn would naturally favour that type of theory. Correspondingly, if they are guided by complete certainty about the future the dreams would fade, the mountains would not seem worth scaling, and even though pushing the stones up new mountains rather than the same mountain as poor old Sisyphus had to do is somewhat more inspiring – there is at least some novelty to the stone pushing – in the longer run it is exasperating to see the stone roll down into the valley again, particularly when one is high enough up to see no limit to the number of mountains ahead. Inaction or the equivalent of this automaton robot action would be the likely consequence – soulless, uninspired ritualism; usually referred to as fatalism. There would be no pursuit; no crystallization, no transcendence.

To be human, somehow, seems to have something to do with living in a spectrum between the positivist and the fatalist options. Actually, they are two different ways of saying the same: it is all written up in a big book, there is little we can do, except knowing what is written in that book and then try to live according to that knowledge. It is not up to us to change the text of the book. What positivism promised was that we could get to read the book, even to write it if we promised to let nature (including human society) dictate what we write by respecting what positively exists, what is. The doctrine would be that from 'what is, is possible' it follows 'what is not, is impossible'. However, the only thing that follows would be that 'what is impossible, is not', which is something different. For there is the potential, the possible, yet not existing – and here positivism is of no help[5].

To this it may be objected that women have known all the time that *some* women have made it, they have even been queens. In other words, there has been that empirical exception that could serve as a guiding light. The relative frequencies have opened for the possibility of *some* hope, there has been *some* uncertainty. But take then the case of children. The present author is absolutely convinced that children have potentials unheard of, underutilized, even totally unused in the social formations best known to us today. Thus, in a society where by some kind of technology basic needs would be guaranteed satisfied, and by some kind of cosmology not more than basic needs satisfaction would be asked for, materially speaking, everybody might be much more interested in playful activity. Would it not be likely that in such societies the children might be the teachers and adults the pupils – particularly adults who had been deformed through participation in highly unplayful social formations? And however this would be, is it not also preposterous to assume that children that are systematically kept away from work (today under the pretext of protecting them from exploitation) would not if they were given a chance of creative (not ritualistic) work activity also develop much more quickly potentials that adults pride themselves of seeing as the prerogative of adults? When are they actually well-protected interests?

Neither positivism, nor fatalism, are the basic epistemologies that explain why humans sometimes transcend: because we are blessed by uncertainty. That uncertainty can be agonizing everybody knows; anybody who has passed some of his life in prison can testify that certainty can be even more agonizing. The kinds of things prisoners do in order to inject an element of uncertainty in otherwise completely predictable environments (such as eating forks and knives, playing with their bodies, even with death, in order to gain some new experience, such as an operation) provide ample testimony to this[6]. And here we are even helped by *two* uncertainties at the same time: the uncertainty as to whether we will win the fight against the heavy odds, *and* the uncertainty about the nature of the goal once we are there: the difference between the mountain as viewed from a distance and the mountain as concrete experience.

Our gift in rejecting positivist and fatalist orientations, our talent in persuading ourselves the chances are not that bad, even of manoeuvring our perceptions into a corner of perfect uncertainty telling ourselves that past experience does not apply in this case, nor the gloomy predictions of those who claim they have explored the social and historical landscape in front of our own forward positions. Thus, if the Third World countries today should really take seriously everything they are told by people from the First World countries about the gloom of overdevelopment, about the social ills of industrial society, they might prefer to do nothing at all, thereby lapsing into non-historical, stationary states. This does not mean that they will blindly follow into all the traps and corners the First World has painted itself into. It only means that a vision of higher material level of living serves as a first guideline, as a basis for one social intuition that inspires action; and that action itself to be questioned as one comes closer. In general there is little reason to worry that actors of any kind will repeat exactly the mistakes of actors they claim they imitate, precisely because of the human talent, and indeed the need to inject uncertainty in their own action. To imitate, to pursue the trajectory of somebody ahead of oneself, is tantamount to fatalism, it means giving away the gift of uncertainty. And in so doing the daring ventures into the unknown out of which new social formations, i.e. transcendence, may ensue will not take place. To make a photocopy is not the same as writing an article – that is why it is wrong to condemn people to photocopying all the time: the certainty of the action kills the transcendence known as personal growth[7].

CONCLUSION

We have been extolling the virtues of uncertainty. Clearly, like anything human, the record sheet of uncertainty is not only positive, nor is it as uncomplicated as it is portrayed above. For one thing, it follows from what has been said that crime cannot be eradicated through increasing detection and conviction probabilities: human beings are not made that way. We are capable of transforming certainties into uncertainties, perhaps even more so the more 'rational' judgment should inspire very literal interpretations of the past as guidelines for the future. People may abstain from, or not engage in, crime for other reasons: they may simply not want it, get what they want by other means or – possibly the most important anti-mechanism – not be imaginative or daring enough. (Incidentally, if crime is for the daring and the imaginative they may be particularly skilful in transforming knowledge into belief, doing the opposite of what the more stolid and solid bureaucrats and researchers who theorize about them might have done.)

This also applies to the concept of incompatibility: not only is uncertainty as to the outcome a necessary condition for risk-taking in situations of contradiction and conflict; uncertainty about the incompatibility is also important. Take the 'incompatibility' between work and enjoyment: for he who has work the outcome of which has an element of uncertainty work may be a source of enjoyment, but also of pain, agony; it is only when the work is surrounded by certainties in all directions that – at least after a while – it becomes almost certain that it is incompatible with enjoyment.

In this there is also a reason why the regimes in Eastern Europe do not seem to work very well: *there is that dream of the surprise-free society*. Planning is reduction of uncertainty and there is no argument here that there is no scope for planning: there are uncertainties we can do without (e.g. relating to earthquakes; they could be transformed into certainties that they will not occur without that certainty causing much harm). But the perfectly planned, benevolent society is in for greater surprises than the malevolent society ridden with uncertainties: people will *create* uncertainties, although, admittedly, many of them may be in the spiritual rather than in the material sphere (a reason why people nevertheless seek the agony of uncertainty of salvation in materially guaranteed countries).

In short: Do not take uncertainties away from us humans. They can be overdone, but they are the material out of which human and social development are made.

NOTES

1. Carnap's expression is as rational as Carnap himself seems to be as judged from his books. People like Carnap are probably poor guides to how most of humanity experiences phenomena like 'probability' – at least they should conduct much experimental research in order to have their prejudgments checked with some touch of reality.
2. Von Mises, in his important work, did the job of giving the study of probability its positivist touch – but it is remarkable how the notion of probability, like God, democracy, liberty and what-not, even socialism, seems to survive all efforts at definition.
3. Laplace, borrowing from the general *ars conjectandi* tradition, was probably much too much influenced by dice and by the idea that true, honest dice are not biased – when there is deviation from equiprobability something dishonest or wrong is at work!
4. See, for example, the otherwise excellent book edited by Peter Hall (1977) which predicts and prescribes future states but not the action leading to them. What kind of attitude will the book engender in the reader? A feeling that this is probably going to happen anyhow – hence no action is needed? A desire to work out for himself, and herself, the missing links, the actions required? The question is whether people want to work out actions if the consequences are too well known in advance – a basic problem for all concerned with future studies.
5. For a development of this theme see my Chapter on 'Empiricism, Criticism, Constructivism' in Galtung (1977).
6. See Galtung (1957) for an analysis of what prisoners do in one particular prison to decrease certainty, and see also Cohen (1970).
7. For the general theory of conflict underlying some of the reflections in this paper, see *Theories of Conflict*, (forthcoming) – a work originally started upon the encouragement of John Cohen and so far only twelve years behind schedule – a good example of uncertainty at work. But the gratitude to John Cohen for having asked me to undertake the task is as great as ever and, like

the man who always says "it is twelve o'clock", the person who, like me, says "forthcoming" may also eventually be proven right. My indebtedness to the work of John Cohen is clear from this paper, both to the many papers from his hand and to the particularly instructive introduction to his type of thinking as found in Cohen and Christensen (1970).

BIBLIOGRAPHY

Cohen, J. (1970). Uncertainty and risk-taking in crime. *Bulletin of the British Psychological Society*, **23**, 293–296

Cohen, J. and Christensen, I. P. (1970). *Information and Choice.* (Edinburgh: Oliver and Boyd)

Galtung, J. (1957). *Fengselssamfunnet.* (*The Prison Community*). (Oslo)

Galtung, J. (1977). *Methodology and Ideology.* (Copenhagen: Ejlers)

Hall, P. (1977). *Europe 2000.* (London: Duckworth)

Subject Index

Bibliographic references shown in **bold** type.

Index of Names